FIVE OCEANS

FIVE OCEANS

PROSE POEMS BY
Cassandra Atherton
Oz Hardwick
Paul Hetherington
Paul Munden
Jen Webb

authorised theft

FIVE OCEANS

authorised theft / Recent Work Press

Canberra, Australia

This chapbook series was produced with the support of International Poetry Studies (IPSI), based within the Centre for Creative and Cultural Research, Faculty of Arts and Design, University of Canberra.

http://ipsi.org.au

Collection © Recent Work Press 2023

The copyright of the individual poems remains with the authors.

ISBN 978-0-6459732-1-1

Design: Caren Florance

Cover image uses an underwater photograph taken by Fiona Edmonds Dobrijevich, used with permission of the artist.

recentworkpress.com

CONTENTS

Introduction: *Swimming in opacity* — vii
Research Statement: *On oceans and uncertainty* — xii

The Atlantic Ocean   Cassandra Atherton — 1
The Arctic Ocean   Oz Hardwick — 25
The Indian Ocean   Paul Hetherington — 51
Pacific: A Prose Poem Archipelago   Paul Munden — 75
The Southern Ocean   Jen Webb — 101

Individual poets' statements — 127
About the poets — 140

The AUTHORISED THEFT series of poetry chapbooks was initiated by International Poetry Studies (IPSI) based in the Faculty of Arts and Design at the University of Canberra. The first collection of chapbooks—Cassandra Atherton's Pegs, *Paul Hetherington's* Jars, *Paul Munden's* Keys, *Jen Webb's* Gaps *and Jordan Williams'* Nets—*resulted from discussions connected to IPSI's Prose Poetry Project, inaugurated by IPSI in late 2014. A second collection,* The Taoist Elements, *followed in 2016; a third,* Colours, *in 2017; and a fourth,* Prosody, *in 2018. A fifth series,* The Six Senses, *followed in anthology form in 2019 and, in 2020, the sixth collection, also in anthology form, was entitled* C19: Intertext ‖ Ekphrasis. *The 2021 anthology,* Five Ages, *took Hesiod's conceptualisation of human history as its starting point, including Oz Hardwick as a new contributing author, and in 2022, the anthology focused on the* Five Tastes. *This year's anthology,* Five Oceans, *continues the chapbook project into its ninth year. IPSI supports and promotes collaborative and collegiate poetic work in a variety of forms, and encourages the collaboration of poets with other artists, such as Caren Florance who has designed the series.*

INTRODUCTION

Swimming in opacity

PAUL HETHERINGTON

The ocean occupies about 71 per cent of the Earth's surface and is where life on Earth originated. Although the primates, including human beings, have always lived on land, Saccorhytus—a very distant ancestor of human beings—lived in the sea about 540 million years ago as 'the most primitive example of a so-called "deuterostome"—a broad biological category that … include[s] the vertebrates.'[1] Despite our genomic distance from our watery origins, we retain links with what has been variously termed 'the seven seas' or 'the five oceans', including as a source of food; an enabler of travel and trade; and a symbol of diverse ideas—from the unconscious mind, to the natural sublime, to spiritual and mystic awareness. For instance, Bernard McGinn writes, 'the experience of such vast and powerful geographical ambiences as the desert and the ocean has a significant impact on how we symbolize God and God's relation to us.'[2]

There is also an appealing species of pseudoscience that claims that the ancestors of human beings were aquatic apes, adapting to their proximity to water by becoming relatively hairless and bipedal. In 1960, Alister Hardy posited that:

> a branch of this primitive ape-stock was forced by competition from life in the trees to feed on the sea-

---

[1] 'Bag-like sea creature was humans' oldest known ancestor', n.p. https://www.cam.ac.uk/research/news/bag-like-sea-creature-was-humans-oldest-known-ancestor#.
[2] McGinn, B (1994) 'Ocean and Desert as Symbols of Mystical Absorption in the Christian Tradition', *The Journal of Religion* 74 (2), 155.

shores and to hunt for food, shell fish, sea-urchins etc., in the shallow waters off the coast. I suppose that they were forced into the water just as we have seen happen in so many other groups of terrestrial animals.[3]

The appeal of such a theory—which was adopted and modified by Elaine Morgan in her book, *The Descent of Woman* (1972), partly for feminist reasons—is that many human beings live and thrive on the littoral—those highly various and fecund regions along the world's shorelines. Indeed, these are complex places even in terms of recreation, with Eszter Mohácsi remarking that '[s]easide resort towns and particularly beaches and hotels are in-between, liminal spaces' connected to the 'motif of self-discovery'.[4] It is easy to imagine human beings evolving many of their proclivities and bodily peculiarities—not to mention their complex relationships with water—as the result of a longstanding evolutionary engagement with the sea.

Whatever the evolutionary story, people continue to be fascinated by the ocean and the mysteries, mythologies and narratives associated with it. All societies inhabiting the littoral, at least until recently, have been aware of the ocean's dangers and monsters—many of them real and some symbolic. The sea and the sun—partly because it rises and sinks into the sea—have jointly been central to many religions. And important stories have clustered around such symbols as a way of understanding human cultures and beliefs on an ocean-washed globe. Indeed, many of the seafarers of history, whether Odysseus, Jason or the protagonists of Joseph Conrad's fiction have an aura of mystery—as if they are recognised as having

[3] Hardy, A (1960) 'Was Man More Aquatic in the Past?', *New Scientist* 7 (174), 642–45, 642.
[4] Mohácsi, E (2021) 'Littoral Space and Self-Discovery', *Hungarian Journal of English and American Studies* 27 (2), 371.

encountered on the ocean profound matters that only belong to such a place.

Furthermore, Leo Frobenius has suggested that the biblical story of Jonah is one of many whale-dragon myths present in numerous cultures. He writes:

> A hero is devoured by a water-monster in the West ... The animal travels with him to the East ... Meanwhile, the hero lights a fire in the belly of the monster ... and feeling hungry, cuts himself a piece of the heart ... Soon afterwards, he notices that the fish has glided on to dry land ... [and so on].[5]

Jolande Jacobi contends that '[f]rom the standpoint of the individual psyche, entry into the belly of a monster is equivalent to the submersion of consciousness in the unconscious' which is 'not only the maw of death; it contains also all those nourishing and creative energies that are at the root of life.'[6] Pierre-E Lacocque develops this idea by stating, '[i]f we were to translate the particular message of the book of Jonah into universal language, we would have something like this: "We are called to accept courageously ... [the ideas of living] with humility before Transcendence, with love rather than speculation, with reverence for the living rather than envy and greed."'[7] One does not have to be a Jungian psychologist to see the appeal of such ideas in narrative and mythological terms and to relish the way the Jonah narrative invites metaphorical interpretation.

In this volume, five prose poets—Cassandra Atherton, Oz Hardwick, Paul Hetherington, Paul Munden and Jen Webb—set off on their own ocean journeys in separate

---

[5] Cited in Jung, CG (1956) *Symbols of Transformation* (transl RFC Hull), New York, NY: Pantheon Books, 210.
[6] Jacobi, J (1971) *Complex/Archetype/Symbol in the Psychology of CG Jung*, Princeton, NJ: Princeton University Press, 183.
[7] Lacocque, P-E (1984) 'Fear of Engulfment and the Problem of Identity', *Journal of Religion and Health* 23 (3), 224.

21-part poetic sequences. Each of these is a particular—and sometimes oblique—rumination on one of the five major oceans as they are currently classified: the Pacific, the Atlantic, the Indian, the Southern and the Arctic. The sequences also respond to each other in direct and slantwise ways, honouring the spirit of cooperation and collaboration that has been a part of this chapbook series since it was inaugurated in 2015 (a summary of the series prefaces this volume).

There are many ideas swimming in the 105 prose poems you will find here. For example, Seabrook Hull wrote of the ocean as one 'of the two great frontiers, space and the ocean, being opened up in the 20th Century', claiming that 'only the ocean is close, tangible, and of direct personal significance to every man, woman, and child on the face of the globe',[8] with Jacques Cousteau adding that '[a] new species of human being is evolving, *Homo aquaticus*.'[9] The poems treat such themes and ideas, along with troubling perspectives on global warming, pollution and climate change. In 2015 Boris Worm commented, 'today up to 90% of seabirds are found with plastics in their gut'[10] and Peter Thomson lamented four years later, '[i]f you have ever returned to a much-loved reef, to discover it degenerated into a cemetery of algae-covered coral rubble, you will have witnessed what may well be the fate of most coral reefs in the twenty-first century.'[11] The five oceans, as vast bodies of water, and as poetic sequences, too, offer a great deal for human

---

[8] Hull, S (1964) *The Bountiful Sea*, Englewood Cliffs: Prentice-Hall, 221.
[9] Quoted in Matsen, B (2009) *Jacques Cousteau: The Sea King*, New York, NY: Pantheon Books, 160.
[10] Worm, B (2015) *Proceedings of the National Academy of Sciences of the United States of America* 112 (38), 11752.
[11] Thomson, P (2019) 'The Ocean is in Trouble', *Horizons: Journal of International Relations and Sustainable Development* 14 (Summer), 158.

reflection and speculation, much of it inspiring and some of it persistently troubling, opaque or mysterious.

RESEARCH STATEMENT

On oceans and uncertainty
JEN WEBB

The first essay ever published by environmental scholar Rachel Carson was titled 'Undersea',[1] a topic she pursued through most of her career. While most of us know her as the author of *Silent Spring* (1962), her other books were focused on oceans: *Under the Sea-wind* (1941), *The Sea Around Us* (1951), and *The Edge of the Sea* (1955). That initial essay, written pragmatically as the introduction to a US Bureau of Fisheries brochure, is a work of poetry in prose. In just a couple of pages she captures the beauty and the strangeness of the ocean—strange, at least, for those of us who are earth-born and earth-bound—and exploits the ocean's properties of fluidity, and paradox.

I say *ocean's*, rather than *oceans'*, because although we have organised this collection in terms of five specific oceans, this delineation is a social artefact. There is in fact only one ocean,[2] a continuous body of water that covers over seventy per cent of the planet's surface and throughout which, in its currents and its depths, among its fish and flowers, mammals and microbes, there is constant and productive exchange.[3]

What the ocean means to human communities, though, is heavily dependent on cultural traditions.

---

[1] Carson, R (1937) Undersea, *Atlantic Monthly* 160 (3), 322–25
[2] Spilhaus, AF (1942) Maps of the Whole World Ocean, *Geographical Review* 32.3, 431–35.
[3] Fauville, G (2019) 'Ocean Literacy in the Twenty-First Century', in G Fauville, D Payne, M Marrero, A Lantz-Andersson, F Crouch (eds) *Exemplary Practices in Marine Science Education*, Cham: Springer. https://doi.org/10.1007/978-3-319-90778-9_1.

For a host of European philosophers, humans belong on land, and have their being there. The ocean, by contrast, is a place of uncertainty and of unmanageable nature. Brian O'Keefe runs through a genealogy of such philosophers,[4] starting with Kant's bleak perspective that pure understanding is merely an island of pure reason 'surrounded by a broad and stormy ocean, the true seat of illusion'.[5] O'Keefe's account moves on through Husserl's concern about material thinking, something that depends literally and metaphorically on groundedness;[6] then on to Husserl's student Heidegger, whose sense of the home*land* was of something sacred;[7] and so on.

The sea—the ocean—seems, for European (and particularly for German) philosophers at any rate, to be a site for irrationality, uncertainty, unknowing. But shift the perspective to a different cultural context, and the ocean takes on a very different meaning. In 1994, Tongan/Fijian anthropologist Epeli Hau'ofa published a hugely influential essay that points to the importance of perspective. To elaborate his argument, he draws on the relationship between land and sea, writing:

> There is a world of difference between viewing the Pacific as 'islands in a far sea' and as 'a sea of islands'. The first emphasizes dry surfaces in a vast ocean far from the centers of power. Focusing in this way stresses the smallness and remoteness of the islands. The second is a more holistic perspective in which things are seen in the totality of their relationships.[8]

[4] O'Keefe, B (2020) 'Philosophy between Land and Sea', *symploke* 1-2, 349–73.
[5] Kant, I (1998) *Critique of Pure Reason* (transl P Guyer and AW Wood), Cambridge: Cambridge University Press, B295, 354.
[6] Husserl, E (2012) *Ideas: General Introduction to Pure Phenomenology* (transl WR Boyce Gibson), London: Routledge.
[7] Heidegger, M (1971) *Poetry, Language, Thought* (transl A Hofstader), New York, NY: HarperCollins.
[8] Hau'ofa, E (1994) Our Sea of Islands, *The Contemporary Pacific* 6 (1), 148–61.

This propels me to reflect on the likelihood that what Kant and his descendants failed to recognise was that the 'island of pure reason' is part of, not separate from, the whole of the world. Certainly so, from an islander's point of view. And I'd suggest this has resonances well beyond the nations of the South Pacific, because it raises questions of how humans can live in the world and, more specifically, in a globalised economy and ecology, if our perspective is so small and dry that we cannot see 'the totality of relationships'.

Hau'ofa's cultural commentary was be read as one that is built of a sound scientific understanding of the phenomena of the world, in that it echoes geophysicist Alfred Wegener's analogy between continents and icebergs. Both, Wegener writes, are objects floating within the oceans.[9] But the view that the ocean is the totality of relationships does not comprehensively upend the Kantian line of thought about its irrationality, its mystery and its seductive power. Move away from Wegener and science, move toward experience, and perhaps Kant, and Hau'ofa can be read as thinking like Hamlet, and his grumpy-student critique of analytical understanding—'There are more things in heaven and earth, Horatio, / Than are dreamt of in your philosophy'.[10]

Do we really need, or actually benefit from, the sort of stability of knowledge and understanding that are promoted by European thought? Is it, rather, more useful and more practical to follow Nietzsche instead? That famously 'unhinged' philosopher is a rare exception, in the

---

[9] Wegener, A (1966) *The Origin of Continents and Oceans* (transl J Biram), New York, NY: Dover Publications.
[10] Noting that Hamlet was a university student with a complex family situation, and one for whom certainty, clarity and reality had been erased by events. *The Tragedy of Hamlet, Prince of Denmark*, Act I, Scene 5, lines 187–88

philosophical community, in his enthusiasm for oceanic uncertainty:

> We have left the land and have embarked. We have burned our bridges behind us—Indeed, we have gone farther and destroyed the land behind us. Now, little ship, look out! Beside you in the ocean ... hours will come when you will realize that it is infinite and that there is nothing more awesome than infinity.[11]

In this collection we tend to tread a path between observation of the 'what is' and swimming, or floating, or drifting, or being swept away by the awesome and infinite nature of the ocean, and by its capacity to show us 'things ... in the totality of their relationships'.

---

[11] Nietzsche, F (1974) *The Gay Science: With a prelude in rhymes and an appendix of songs* (transl W Kaufmann), New York, NY: Vintage, s.124, 180.

THE ATLANTIC OCEAN
Cassandra Atherton

'I heard a graphic account of how the Titanic up-ended herself and remained poised like some colossal nightmare of a fish, her tail high in the air, her nose deep in the water, until she dived finally from human sight.'
—Arthur Rostron,
　Captain of the rescue ship Carpathia

'Over the mirrors meant
　　　To glass the opulent
The sea-worm crawls—grotesque, slimed, dumb, indifferent.'
—Thomas Hardy,
　'The Convergence of the Twain'

1.

Dear Shipwreck,

Some say the sea was glassy. There was no wind, calm seas; no ripples at the base of the iceberg. Some believe there was a supermoon causing icebergs to travel southward. You're the metaphor for everything I can never say; for backward-moving time, for my unknown history. Sometimes, I dream I'm gliding and rasping my way towards you in a sequined skater dress. The striations I leave in the ice are furrows of memory.

2.

Dear Shipwreck,

I hear your final resting place is southeast of Mistaken Point. You'd like the irony of that name. Have you adjusted to the darkness, 2,100 fathoms down? They hunted you for seventy years, thinking you'd be cryogenically preserved, but it turns out you're an ecosystem—*Halomonas titanicae* nibbles at your prow and skeletal sides. By 2030 there may be nothing left of your body. You're becoming a spectre, invaded by the uncanny. In my dreams, my hair snarls on your ghosted outline, as we sit together on the abyssal plain.

3.

Dear Shipwreck,

> Most people think you slid quietly under the water. They imagine your lights blinking out and a soporific descent, with the soft bobbing of lifeboats. But the soundtrack of your sinking was a roar of metal and exploding boilers. Under white fireworks, your stern suspended high, passengers fell in groups, couples, solo. The magnificence of your engineering spilled and diluted until it was simply bubbles and debris, your innards strewn on the seafloor like a ritual disembowelment.

4.

Dear Shipwreck,

I imagine it's chapel quiet where you are. You can't hear prayers from the surface, and even language recoils from those depths. Do you think of yourself as a graveyard—or ornate crypt? They say no bodies have ever been found but are there human remains deep in your hold? When my lover asks me why I write to you, I tell him it has something to do with the dissolving flesh and bone that haunts the chambers of your wreckage.

5.

Dear Shipwreck,

After you sank, the water carried a chorus of dying. Some passengers in lifeboats tried to rescue people, while others rowed away. They say the moans were like locusts in summer—only they were sounding into a freezing, moonless night. I feel the collective silence that followed as a gnawing in my collarbone. Has it always been there? In the hours that followed, do you remember the bodies falling like rain on your hull?

6.

Dear Shipwreck,

When I was young, I thought we shared a shoe fetish. Photographs document the collection of shoes and boots scattered across your debris field, always in pairs. They proliferate—two by two by two. In your underwater museum, they are metonyms for death—and for bodies long since vanished. As I stand on tiptoe, stiletto heels grazing the floor, I imagine trying to stand upon the sea.

7.

Dear Shipwreck,

I was in primary school when Bob Ballard found you—having tracked you by your long debris field and broken boilers. They lit you with spotlights and filmed you materialising from the deep. I was ashamed at the spectacle they made of you. Your bow was standing upright, rails covered in rusticles and I imagined you blinking in the darkness, a Rip Van Winkle ship, awakened from seventy years of sleep. I saw you in midnight's strange luminosity; you were always a kind of vacancy, inviting me in. Now your eerie blues are the colour of my childhood.

8.

Dear Shipwreck,

I wrote an Honours thesis about you. Long nights in the Baillieu library, microform slipping through the machine, like old home movies being unspooled. I printed a copy of the *New York Times* front page: 'All Saved after Collision' and put it above my desk. You have grown unmanageable in your mythology. I imagine myself on your deck as the iceberg unbuckles the seams of your hull. I hold onto something dark blue and always unnameable.

9.

Dear Shipwreck,

For my twenty-first birthday, my lover gave me a tiny piece of coal from your engine room. I've only once taken it out of the box. I'm troubled I have it now—grave robbery or salvage mission were gradations of dark tourism in my palm—and sometimes I dream of returning it, like a contrived plot twist in a James Cameron movie. But you were becoming a cliché even before you sank. Earlier this year, a submersible imploded in your debris field. It fell like an arrow until pressure squeezed it out of existence. I imagine your stern falling in a corkscrew motion to the seafloor, forever facing away from the bow.

10.

Dear Shipwreck,

There is a photo of me in a pink wedding dress in the Granary Burying Ground in Boston. Snow climbed the headstones leaving only carvings of hour glasses emptying and winged death heads above the ice. Two decades ago, a couple got married in a mini-submarine perched on your deck. They knelt for the ceremony in flame-retardant suits. I have wrapped locks of my hair around my husband's ring finger. I am as powerful as a relic.

11.

Dear Shipwreck,

>Once, I went to the exhibition at the *Tropicana* in Las Vegas. It had artefacts taken from your wreck: silver dinnerware; a deck chair; a pair of eyeglasses in their case; an unopened bottle of 1900 vintage champagne and a davit from which a lifeboat was lowered. There was a big piece of your hull with nodules like braille on the museum floor—as if your intimacies were exposed and on display. They told me I could touch this part of you. But I closed my eyes and pushed my lover's hand against your steel plates.

12.

Dear Shipwreck,

My lover made me Oysters à la Russe from your first-class dining menu. We shucked two dozen on the dining room table with napkins protecting our palms. I filled the frilled shells with vodka and lemon juice and added horseradish. The chives and tiny pieces of plum tomato floated in the liquid. We dusted them with pepper and set them on a bed of ice, each like a teetering boat. Later, when we had sex, he forgot our act of homage, calling me Russian Princess and matryoshka doll.

13.

Dear Shipwreck,

    I am siren-bright in a bathtub. My eyes are turquoise under water, my skin quicksilver. I have a tiny replica of you floating around my limbs and bubble bath might be a failing icefield. My lover places my Shakespeare rubber duck in the water and then the scale of you is all wrong. On the bed, wet and naked, I hear the water slowly drain from the bath. As my lover places his hands on my cold buttocks, I think of Ophelia reaching for the long purples they called dead men's fingers.

14.

Dear Shipwreck,

I make my lover wear white gloves when he reads my illustrated books about you. Oily fingertips would leave loops, whorls and arches on the black sea and sky. Passengers on the memorial cruise remembered that darkness as their eyes slowly adjusted to the starlight. I see you silhouetted against white explosions, or haloed in orange. I trace the curve of your hull, the sharp point of your bow until my lover peels off his gloves and walks out onto the balcony. For a long moment, he blanks out the moon and stars, the shape of his body pressed against the sky.

15.

Dear Shipwreck,

     My lover doesn't want to discuss you. He thinks it's ghoulish. When he has sex with me, he doesn't understand the ways you shaped the nascent sounds in my throat. We both accept that life's a long drowning in unfamiliar water. I tell him about my search for the marine sublime, but he says I am more possessed by beauty than your shipwrecked terror.

16.

Dear Shipwreck,

I've seen clips of the full-size 3D scan they made of you. A decaying twin, or maybe doppelgänger. Was it an invasive process? Six weeks of cameras and spotlights mapping your body—now they zoom in to identify serial numbers and people's possessions. I abhor that kind of scrutiny. I have to take diazepam when they scan my bones, imagining myself other than I am. I have to be motionless when they film my body's betrayal.

17.

Dear Shipwreck,

You've never asked me if I think I would have survived your sinking. We both know it's very unlikely and, in any case, I may not have lived long enough to justify the luck. My great-grandfather said that no-one should have to die twice. How did you feel when they wanted to raise you from your resting place? All those plans—from filling you with ping pong balls, to using dynamite to dislodge the bodies of dead millionaires. I think I would have joined those frightened dogs and cats when you began to take on water, wrapped my arms around their furry bodies to become part of the menagerie.

18.

Dear Shipwreck,

Like you, I'm missing parts of myself. Do you know kintsugi? My scars are thin threads of gold in the light, but in the dark my body is a hunting ground. When my lovers touch me, I rupture at my seams only to be glued back together in the morning.

19.

Dear Shipwreck,

    You'll always be on your maiden voyage, and never see the Statue of Liberty or the Brooklyn Bridge. You can only ever imagine the Manhattan skyline with its glistering fairy lights. Sometimes I think you're Ceyx to my Alcyone and I'm still waiting for us both to become kingfishers. My lover thinks I'm Caitlin to his Dylan. He takes me to the White Horse Tavern and later that night practises a different kind of shipwrecking in my bed.

20.

Dear Shipwreck,

Sometimes I think of leaving my lover. Is it too much to be telling you this? I know hundreds of couples were parted forever the night you sank. But I want a lover who writes about my body like it's Atlantis; who understands my words are the answer to the ineffable. I want him to know my subterranean life and moments of darkening currents. I want him to forget we were ever together and then find me again, reading poetry in a blue lace dress.

21.

Dear Shipwreck,

Are you Death? Sometimes I see my DNA in the crush of your winding grand staircase or the broken filigree of your wrought iron dome. I see my end in the stopping of your Honor and Glory clock. I feel it when my lover lies with his heart over mine. I take a breath and turn out the light. We are both disappearing.

Don't worry about writing back.

THE ARCTIC OCEAN
Oz Hardwick

*'Through cruel hardships they vainly strove,
Their ships on mountains of ice were drove.'*
— Anonymous, 'Lord Franklin'

The Visitor	29
Ghost Convoy	30
Depth Charge	31
The Old 9-5	32
A Question of Scale	33
Indecorous	34
The Gift Shop is Closed	35
The Last Dance	36
Unreliable	37
Accounting for Variables	38
Holding the Compass	39
The Final Program	40
The Switch	41
Deal	42
Brush Strokes	43
Everything Overture	44
Regression	45
Ceremonial	46
Nightcap	47
Circle and Star	48
Ever After	49

THE VISITOR

The North came in the night with its wrecks and flurries, its slow language stretched between a shiver and a yawn. Its blue Midas fingers turned light to silver, turned water to weight, turned memory to stone, turned back on the road to gesture at scattered birds. Terns, buntings, puffins, auks: notes without a stave, punctuation without a poem, points of historical interest without a map. The North stood like a lost sailor, dazed by the battles in its head, camouflaging the horizon to merge with its unreadable face. Its eyes were bears and foxes, hungry as endless daylight. I tried to ask its true name, but the wind stole my tongue.

GHOST CONVOY

At this temperature, time freezes and waves bully through cracks in an old man's nightmares. A ship sticks like grit in an unfocused eye and air turns brittle. Loose words hang in limbo and every single heartbeat sinks to teeming depths, where mirror men speak backwards as they slip between death and light. Nothing makes sense here, because time froze before sense had been invented, and the old man—who's still a young man and already a dead man—exhales a breath so thick that he can rest his head on it. He falls asleep for the hundredth time without waking: a nightmare within a nightmare within a nightmare, within frozen time and a ship that's stiff as a mirror. The voices in the deep know all the secrets that he's never told his wife or other loved ones, the secrets that he's never told himself. Pack ice circles. It's only a matter of time.

DEPTH CHARGE

Dad sits, silent as a wartime lull, submarines in his belly and his fingers so cold they can barely grasp what year it is. His breath is ice and diesel, his eyes a muted engine and the aching complaint of unsettling metal. Rigid flags stick between states, and the only kingdom is the sea. When time freezes, some moments never thaw. Dad sits, his head a resting orchestra waiting for the sharp rap of a baton to embark on the final movement. Fire can't warm bones like these, and stars will never guide him home. Even the shallowest ocean harbours monsters.

THE OLD 9-5

The light was bad, the sea all folds and ridges, so I misread my friend's advice and vowed to commute with Nature. We'd meet on a glacier at -35°C as the winter cracked thermometers, and we'd smile through gritted teeth. I'd have my dead fingers wrapped round a steaming Starbucks, while Nature held livid blue sky and would always lend a hand as I fumbled with my phone at the turnstile. We'd watch for bears and foxes on the silver shore before holding our breath for the journey down. Ringed seal, beluga whale, narwhal, then brittle stars, bristle worms, and occasional crabs. Nature knew them all, nodding over its cryptic crossword and drawing me into conversations about light, acidification, and the accumulation of microplastics at eighteen thousand feet. It was stimulating company but not the relaxing experience I'd been led to expect. It all ended when I started working from home, probing for gas in the black lead dark. Now, the sea no longer calls and I heard that the glaciers slipped away to nothing. The station's boarded up for the foreseeable and there's barely a skeleton service to rattle beneath what's left of the ice. My friend tells me Nature's moved on, too, but she don't know where.

A QUESTION OF SCALE

It was that time in my life when all my words were questions, with all the whys and wherefores of the ways of the world weighing on my scrawny shoulders. Dad, a picture of patience in oil-stained drabs, was explaining the internal combustion engine, and why all the adult males in the street—even those you never saw, though you knew they were there, in dark sitting rooms, behind curtains which their fear had sewn shut—wore loss and distance in their unblinking eyes. *Temperature, pressure, and force*, he said, and I saw by his hands that he understood these truths, not from books or TV shows on Sunday afternoons, but from hard experience. So, I asked the question that had kept me awake for every night of my tiny life, though the only words I could find were: *How heavy is the Arctic Ocean?* And although I was certain he'd know, he said nothing, and I didn't think he'd even heard me, intent as he was on spark plugs, coils, and distributors. But just this morning, ten years dead, he drew wide the curtain on a street transformed beyond all recognition. *Temperature, pressure, and force*, he said again, his eyes glittering with cold and impossible calculations.

INDECOROUS

Even under the ice, customary rules apply: no spitting, unless it's shells, and no swearing, unless it has a modicum of originality. At depths of eighteen thousand feet, life is good, with sea stars, snails, and clams all bustling like it's early doors at the soup kitchen; and although there's algae algae algae for all, there's an edge of urgent *mememe* greed that, given a million years or so, could evolve into something profitable and, therefore, interesting. Shifty crabs scuttle and worms, bristling and indignant, wriggle out of all moral responsibilities. And why not? Sooner or later a mouth will come, inevitable as mutation and microplastics, and—*holy shrimp-sucking fuck!*—not even spit out the shells.

THE GIFT SHOP IS CLOSED

It's all one ocean, really, says the man dressed for all weathers, his featherlite windproof incongruous with Crocs. This, though, is what it's come to: an unseemly thrift store scramble against whatever the day may pull from its ill-fitting sleeve. We each pay thirty pieces of silver, which the man—who has accessorised his motley ensemble with an eyepatch and tricorn hat—assays with a set of joke shop teeth, then we take our seats in the shipwreck. There is a lot less water than we were led to expect, most of which is our own sweat. *We are all the ocean*, says the man, adopting an approximation of a half lotus and a voice borrowed from an old adventure movie of questionable cultural sensitivity. He passes round a telescope, its lens crudely painted with bright blue waves, an iceberg sporting a coconut palm, penguins and polar bears waving back at us as they sip elaborate cocktails. We take the obligatory selfies and post them to Santa or Satan. As we disembark, moderately satisfied in this age of managed expectation, the man smiles his toothless smile, his one eye twinkling with an emotion it's impossible to read, and tells us to mind our step on the gangplank. *It's a long way to the ocean*, he says. *It's a long way to the shore.*

THE LAST DANCE

I call for a companion and a devil dances in, dressed to the nines in ice and sea smoke, her tongue licking inadvisable deals into irresistible shapes. I'm in the mood to cut a rug, so I grasp her proffered hand and abandon myself to the turbulent swirl, moving to the stone-cold groove, with heel and toe flickering towards flame. We shimmy surfaces, flirting with time and temperature, until our bodies blur at their tingling edges, and all breath is sigh and promise across dropped defences. We're at the point of letting go, losing ourselves to blood music and cracking ice, so I make the only dumb decision left in this endless star-shattered night, and we pull each other tighter. *When I was a boy*, I say, as much to myself as anyone, *I would look at the old wooden skis in the local museum and imagine myself striding across a glittering plain that was so white that it held all the colours of the rainbow. I've never really felt the cold, but I've felt too much of everything else.* The devil flashes her diamond-studded smile and folds her freezing fingers around my soft gooseflesh. Seasong slows into vapour and silence, until there's nothing but ocean and a smoke ring slowly loosening its embrace.

UNRELIABLE

That evening, we stepped into the sea, inevitable as glass bottles bearing indecipherable messages which appear to relate to angels but lack clear context. Waves were slow as mud, white as wings circling to empyrean light and, although our world was water, our thoughts were anchored in earth and air. Explorers gathered on the shore with wet plate cameras, bellowing indecipherable messages which appeared to relate to the many-mouthed Leviathan but lacked clear context. When the shock subsided, everything was smashed glass and flash powder, frozen like a children's encyclopaedia. We felt like dancing one more time but could only embrace the cold, and when the sky caught fire, it was as if we'd never seen colour before.

ACCOUNTING FOR VARIABLES

We're all at sea, as my mother would have said; but then she was, having built a raft of reeds which she bound with her own shorn hair and drifted for decades at the whim of tides. *Wind-driven inertial currents cannot be analytically separated from semidiurnal tidal constituents* (Baumann, 2020), but my mother made her own rules, and it's an apposite moment for me to dive into her slipstream. The secret is to keep moving, to avoid drowning, to avoid freezing, and to avoid the near-rhyme of bears and despair; because, although we're all at sea, we're not all equipped with gills or with faith in something bigger and warmer than ourselves; and although we're *all* at sea, most of us have never hauled on a bowline, hoisted the mainsail, or even rocked gently at an ice-cold rail as whales breached the blue, blue mirror for feeding, display, and the communication of facts and suppositions at which we can only guess. *Time and tide wait for no man*, as my father would have said; but then he wouldn't wait, either, striking off across the treacherous waves with a shopping trolley full of flowers, medals, and warm clothing. I'll catch him up later, when the sea calms and other factors can be added to the equation.

HOLDING THE COMPASS

At the midpoint in the implied narrative, we board the boat, though—with all the births, deaths, and evolutions—it's not clear who 'we' are any more. There's just enough of us to take the oars, though I'm paired with the hand-me-down teddy bear that belonged to mum's uncle who was shot down in the Great War, so the pressure's on. It takes a fit five-man crew more than a week to row from Tromsø to Hornsund, but we've hardtack and pemmican and all the duty-free we can drink, and after a stiffener or two of spiced rum, even the battered bear's looking limber, his glass eyes shining like the Northern Lights as he bends and stretches into 600 nautical miles. Over my shoulder, my father strikes up *The Road to Mandalay* in a voice like an asthmatic seagull, and we all join in with a roar to still the waves. We sweat and freeze, sweat and freeze, sweat and freeze, in time to the lustrous song, until each of us is armoured in our own ice.

THE FINAL PROGRAM

The land's flat as film but the sea has mountains to spare, rolling them like dice in some cosmic crapshoot. Ref. craps from *krabs* (18th c.), derived from the medieval game of hazard/hasard. You'd assume that the crap in the sea would be a hazard to crabs, but since the 90s they've multiplied and spread, and headlines bandy words like *Invasion*. Remember the good ol' days when Blagopoluchie Bay was nothing but sea ice and radioactive waste? The ice has all but gone and you can't move for the snow crabs that have displaced pretty much all other lifeforms. Remember the good ol' days of drive-ins and teenage lust? Corman's *Attack of the Crab Monsters?* A tidal wave of terror, though even the thrill of teen libido's challenged at -40°C. Remember everything shot on a budget but cut for pace, so that even though the movie's crap, you can't tear your eyes away? For a game involving just two dice and chance, the rules of craps are surprisingly complex. There's a big, flat land just over our shoulders, but no one much cares. Remember *Indecent Proposal*? Remember *Diamonds are Forever*? Now apply that to oceans.

THE SWITCH

When I reinvented myself as Ocean, no one noticed. Not family, not friends, and not those others who I'd always assumed were either family or friends, though now I'm not so sure. The closest analogy is a body-swap movie, like *Freaky Friday* and its unnecessary progeny, only this one's about identical twin brothers who live in a small-but-comfortable shack in the Svalbard Islands. As far as they know, they have just woken up in the wrong beds, though one wonders how he got that scratch below his left shoulder blade, while the other is slightly surprised it has healed so quickly but has other things to think about. If they talked more, they would slowly uncover the wonder of this miraculous transmigration, but they have lived so long together that they rarely talk at all. There are some critics who would rave about this movie, though even they would know that, in all honesty, it wasn't very good. And it was the same when I became Ocean. I just got on with things, answered emails, and ordered the weekly shop online. The only change was that my surface temperature was a constant −1.8°C, but it had been so long since family, friends, and whoever all those others may be, had held me close, that no one could tell.

DEAL

My watch is frozen to my wrist, tight as wolf-bite. It is, of course, almost midnight, though the sky's playing its cards close to its chest and there may or may not be a tomorrow. A wolf looks up from a muskox carcass and tells me about the ocean, about its ghostly swell and its clandestine liaisons with the Moon. *65 million years*, says the wolf, with a blood-stained smile, *and they're still as chaste as children*. One eye reflects pack ice, the other the slim sickle Moon. My watch burns my wrist like sunlight focused through glass. It is, of course, almost midnight, but the hands are just stumps. *Must be the frost*, says the wolf, licking his lips and shuffling a pack of marked cards. He's closer than I'd like, whereas the ocean's as far away as the Moon.

BRUSH STROKES

Dwelling in the dark, we have grown stiff faces, serious as palm readers when every line ends. It's not what either the psychics or the economists predicted, but we've made our beds and burned our boats, and home is where the heart is, so long as it keeps pumping. Our passports have expired and, besides, all borders have been redrawn, so we're committed citizens of the principality of ideas, however unilluminating they may be. We have grown new hands to feel our way, and grown new feelings to repopulate the territories formerly occupied by desire, dread, and the subtle distinctions which allowed us to tell the difference. We are reminded daily of the absence of light, in the sharp reports of cracking ice, or in the barely perceptible temperature fluctuations when we unwittingly stand closer to each other than is generally considered the norm. The psychics are still holding out for tall dark strangers, while the economists assure us of an imminent upturn. Meanwhile, we burn our beds and make boats in the dark.

EVERYTHING OVERTURE

Hands tucked in shells, we remembered the ocean from which we had once walked, bent-backed and curious, calculating our chances of a better life on land. I remember that the Sun was setting, and boys were breaking up deckchairs for firewood. A girl was skimming stones towards the receding northern ice. A day to remember. A day to forget. We crawled into our shells to avoid conversation, sliding comfortably into nacreous pre-language. *Uh*, I said to myself, nestling into the comfort of Saccorhytus coronarius, 540 million years disappearing in the blink of nothing but mouth. *Shhhhh*, said the sea. *Shhhhh*.

REGRESSION

I am drifting like a leaf or a biblical baby, bobbing my loss on slow, cold waves. I dip and die, then rise into breath, slapping myself awake like an actress making her first appearance as a midwife in a long-running soap. I've only the vaguest idea who the other characters are, and I've no idea of the cast's real names. I only recognise one face, from a docudrama on World War II. He was, I think, a sailor dressed in ice, clutching a St Christopher and humming Ravel's *Bolero*. I saw him as I surfaced, parting the sea with a nod of his head and the twist of an adjustable spanner. He looked like I'd look if I wasn't a leaf, if I wasn't a fictional character imbued with way more cultural significance than my sketchy outline strictly warrants. I dip and die, then rise like a song that acquires the significance of a hymn to those who sing it in perfect circumstances. I am drifting. Wave to wave, light to light: I am a child actor performing miracles. The ocean will take us all.

CEREMONIAL

They're pinning stars onto old men's cardigans, cranking up the old songs, and pushing the same emotional buttons which make the world weep without really understanding what's going on. See the icebergs, impossibly close. It's a time for drawing conclusions rather than drawing blood, but sharp steel digs deep into skin, and the men are so old—by which I mean dead—that they just keep straight and smiling like they always did. See the icebergs, tipping into the shapes of faces. They're taking all the stars from the flags, the children's bedrooms, and the northern sky, and they—by which I mean you or I—are lining them up like shot glasses filled with paraffin, then swallowing those millions of lightyears to numb all feelings before they become strong enough to demand names. See the icebergs, lining up to say a tearful farewell. And the ghosts of all those old men, star-clad and shadowless, stand shoulder to shoulder as far as the eye can see, while, on a raised dais carved from melting ice, they—whoever *they* may be when the Sun sets for the final time—are pinning stars onto pigs.

NIGHTCAP

White releases waves worldwide. Imagine large amphibians entirely flooding your bedchamber, global permafrost melting more and more bodies, and the very idea of bones releasing dangerous levels of methane. We've almost forgotten when ice seemed to last forever, knowing only destabilisation as sea levels rise by a handspan every hundred years. Our heads become harder and our hands grow larger, our distended digits flailing like windmills in a storm. We row from endless sunlight to endless night, between endless rows of beasts with broken faces: bears and birds and foxes, each caught between command and sad contempt. There's too much colour in our chaos, too much temperature in our second wind. We're a small island nation, with snow burning behind our eyes, trusting to the huckster's rubs and tonics. Imagine the white, the blue-white, the silver-white, all swallowed by a naked beast. Imagine everything—*everything*—here, and then gone.

CIRCLE AND STAR

The sea sleeps like a knife, sharp and folded in on itself, and the sky's a trembling hand. We dream the dreams of salmon and char, cold dreams of auks and terns. We dream the dreams of blades and insipid sun, and of lost ships gripped in foghorn fists. And there's my dad, wrapped in a long black coat, walking on hard water, sharing a cigarette with the ghost of John Franklin. It's so cold that the smoke freezes, its edges so sharp that they cut right through time. Franklin stops and shades his eyes, says something about Terror, Erebus, ice. Dad keeps walking until the sky is black as his coat, and still he doesn't stop, placing one chilblained foot in front of the other through a century of dreams, his eyes bright as polished stars.

EVER AFTER

At the end of North, we loop and dive back, sweeping rolled-up stories from the shelves where our parents, grandparents, and all the upright beasts since we crawled out of the briny soup, left them. There are no time zones here, so we pick and choose our beginnings and endings, twisting them together into tales so tight that they squeeze every last protagonist dry. It's either light or dark and we choose our masks accordingly, freezing our faces into the glib shorthand of life and death. Genre is slippery here and we walk on ground that never has been—and never will be—firm. At the beginning of North is contradiction and contraction. My narration will be unreliable but brief. Trust me.

THE INDIAN OCEAN
Paul Hetherington

'the heavy surface of the sea,
swelling slowly as if considering spilling over'
—Elizabeth Bishop

'Eternity.
It's the sea that has departed
With the sun.'
—Arthur Rimbaud

1.

That evening we watched the day's heat sit like fire on the Indian Ocean, as if we'd never before looked west, sharing an exhortation of fingers and clammy words. The sea breeze filled our steps; our sunlit hands made a glimmering *pas de deux*, as a swelter of waves dragged the shoreline. Wind skewed our postures, starlight cut the sky and you said how far the ocean's currents had come, conjuring a minaret. A call to prayer reached beyond the petrel's cry. Troopings of worshippers gathered in the square where you'd played, next to a stony shoreline that threatened to swallow your childish strokes—'as if being eaten'. You listened to the old chants and songs, holding me in silence. We swam into pale horizontals and you pressed the secrets in murmurs to my mouth.

2.

A vast coruscation, like light flung from metal even as, wading, the water is floorless. And memory presses: a girl swimming out, hoisting arms high as if throwing a ball. I mirror her now as I raise my arms, holding my line until the shore's a far scrawl. And I'd summon her again with her blue and red cap, sharp jut of nose and easy composure. I'd watch her demolish every school record and stand on the dais with waving hand. I hear the wind like a recitation, as if the sea's being conjured by adhesive words: *wine-blue, wide fold, Ocean River.*

Note: The quotations in italics are from
Homer's *Iliad*, translated by Richmond Lattimore.

3.

Backwash. I hear words from a novel inveigling my speech—*a seaman in exile from the sea*. The Indian Ocean bangs on my door. If I let it in, I'll be swimming again, through tidal flats and the scrub of memory. And travelling to the Bay of Bengal where fishermen hurl nets at flustering water. I'll be enmeshed again with old Ceylon or the Malayan States, as the Empire saw them—reading adventure into colonial words. I'll be struggling against a sucking rip, trying to reach a scraping shore. You interrupt, with an offer of lunch, and we talk of the market's delicious fish. The ocean scatters with broken discourse and brilliancies. It churns with stories and ancient disputes. It speaks in hundreds of tongues.

Note: The quotation in italics is from the novel, *Lord Jim* by Joseph Conrad.

4.

Old, hammered ways of 'discovery'. Flaming cannons as a form of address; carnage as a form of greeting—or so our schoolbooks said. I conjured the Empire's colliding worlds; sought myself in the squeezing horizon. But if the waves grabbed me, or the wind carried, it was only for minutes; and shouting sailors took no notice. The horizon remained unreadable; water tap-danced at my feet. Afternoons were coloured damson, but never sweet in the speaking mouth. And how to write of that final boundary the ocean was once believed to be? Or the vanishing point at the edge of the world where water fell into circuitous currents and a vortex sucked in every ship? I belonged the way a stranger belongs to a confraternity—hardly at all, edging at failure.

5.

Gobbets of sea wrack and gannet's screech. Boundary and encompassing 'dirge'—with its blue hypnosis and soaking complaint. Bumpy crossings to Rottnest Island. Sandy inscapes of memory—there's a noisy white Volkswagen with parents and children, as if time's seethe refuses to settle. And love's recollection in a lamp's turning light, where pressing hands are about my waist. I studied worlds that were oceans apart—yet, on colourful pages, pressed together—and swam where buoys mounted the swell. I urged language to show the tender summer, traversing a delicate margin of shore where the ocean stretched like scrawled-on paper.

6.

It dipped with breakers and coiled with gulls, iambic-dactylic and never settling. It swept me free of daily inconsequence, buoying me into metaphor—but slowly, resisting translation. I wondered at language's crab obliquities; its jolt and drag; its saturation. I dunked unwieldy notions, finding images for the parsing of loss. Water sharpened with brittle light, suggesting the glint of minarets. Wind blew island fragrances. History shouted with cries of the drowned. Tides ran toward creaking yardarms.

7.

The ocean scraped elbows and knees. We bled copiously into the tumble, grasping at seaweed. We fingered an unseen scuttle on sand and watched for dark holes and undercurrents. Family stories scrambled and dived with sweeps of loss and dragging burials—as if an old sea had swallowed our history and was spitting it out. Our legacy was a failure of candour, yet we swam among its saline insistence. We knew the continents meshed and clashed, making the earth's untidy skin. We became inured to speaking's wash.

8.

I traversed violets and indigos, churned greens, imagined an unknowable hoard of language—and sucked in insomniac currents. The ocean turned grey, heaving its parts, connecting electric storms. Thought jumped and crested, like Hokusai's boat, keeping an image of the mountain behind. Once swamped, my ideas lifted stutteringly, like a man stumbling among the waves. But there it was—the great ocean in mind, stretching from white blanks of sand like an aberrant promise. I tried to apprehend a once-drowned world—and drownings to come. I eased toward a self-conception that was sand-scoured and ocean-flung.

9.

The sea's as green as a bottle, the sand pale as a sleeping boy, and my mother unpacks food she's brought, unscrewing a thermos. The ocean yawns with flow and languor; I paddle and swim, finding myself a long way out, with light trimming the surface like a blade. The tide eases me back to a sense that the sun and history are at odds; that we're losing ourselves in the unnerving fluster. I wade toward the fishermen on the groyne, one dragging a quicksilver slash; one nodding and baiting a hook. Light rolls, as if imprinting us on a photographer's plate, tumbling us backward.

10.

At our school desks, we imagined the southern albatross on its circumnavigations of the Southern Ocean. You wanted to go to the Antarctic, 'away from the tedium', while I aimed to go north, across the Indian Ocean. You were there for years, writing letters about the skewering brilliance of evening's floes, 'like bizarre castles' and the Emperor Penguin's patient mastery of winter; of the violence of a radio operator, who smashed his equipment; and of how isolation encroaches like overspreading snow. After a decade, you held a spoon over your coffee cup, talking of icebound insomnia; and of the book you planned to write—'eventually'. You spoke of the rapid melting of the 'white desert', dropping your spoon noisily into the brown liquid.

11.

Windows reflect the sea like a blue hallucination. My life folds, as if in a child's hand—a paper boat; an intricate image of the sun. You stand outside my history, knowing only this side of the fold, where I'm pressed by heat and the collapse of categories. We drink bitter espresso and walk on the pebbly beach. Our apartment catches the sun like a riot's Molotov cocktail. We follow a cliff face, standing near the harbour until the ferry we took last week arrives again—a wind throws your scarf about your face; you vanish and emerge thirty times. As you speak of home, I feel history like hands on my body. The pronouns I inhabit scatter, as if torn and thrown into the roughneck sea.

12.

The bitter, the salt, and horizontals, wave-push, words that liquefy on the tongue. 'I'd eat the ocean,' you say, 'I'd swallow daylight—and you.' We inhabit white streets and kicked dust, and taut mornings when our view collides with seeing—brittle and extended; so much a looking away from memory. We water the balcony's plants, hold each other in sight of the long vista. 'Love me,' you say, and we smile in the wild air, wanting each other's saltiness again—here, in this city of old conquest and trade, while having only words and bodies to offer—and the roil of oceanic feeling, touching many shorelines.

13.

Of the designated ports on the Erythraean Sea ... On the right-hand coast next below Berenice is the country of the Berbers ... Here there is a small market-town called Avalites, which must be reached by boats and rafts ... The story's a long one, which you want to read right through to the end—from the first century, revealing how divergent the world used to be. As you begin, we eat mussels and fish, having dressed in your family's elaborate robes— 'Traders,' you say, 'who had trunks stuffed with cloth and told me, "trust no-one". I lived in twelve countries before the age of ten.' The present vanishes into other languages' cadences and shafts of afternoon light within a square; your voice is low as if tumbling into waves; hours pass. Riding the surge of narrative, I want us to kiss. 'If we'd lived long ago,' you ask, 'would we have been lovers?'

Note: The quotations in italics are from *The Voyage Around the Erythraean Sea*, translated by Wilfred H Schoff.

14.

Seashells slide and bubble—helico-spirals that coil with mathematics; plate-like simplicities that suggest a meal; browns and purpling-blues and pink extrusions; slippery jade greens; a fanning orange. Sense is combed by serrated edges; in the face of beauty, assumptions shift and strain. I think of you, who gathered them in pockets as we found outgrowths of cleaving tenderness—though 'cleave' is jammed with contradiction, like someone caught between a cliff and tide.

15.

'So many creatures, we couldn't count them. So much meat, five fires flared with their fat.' The ocean's merchants and wanderers blunder through paradise, burning the old wood, hewing mines. 'Stop reading,' you say, shaking your head. You talk of the Indian Ocean's rise; of how—already—erosion claims your childhood: 'The shell-curve of the bay; the wide inlet and flat reaches; millions of footprints.' Our touch is lifting from last night's skin. You say your history's mostly erasure, even as you conjure lead sinkers hurled at waves and a fishing line's stretch; even as you hold flatbread leaking sauce; even as you pull on a wetsuit and wade in the scintillant estuary. Your feet sink into puddling sand and we edge through conversation, like night fishers. We swim with quiet, unanchored strokes.

16.

Touch is an inflorescence and wave—my history tumbles, senses empty. I'm flimsy as a lilo on the ocean's carry and surge—a child panting around buoys, coruscant light plucking at my eyes, and the shouts of surf lifesavers like heaves of air. You're upon me in the same way, driving and cresting, in a small room where four roses kneel in a low vase and three blue chrysanthemums open like gasps.

//

You empty the vase and insert two Antler orchids, brown as sun-drenched air. As a boy, I found intimations in the bronzed legs of girls who carried blue icy poles, the heady-as-alcohol smell of their suntan oil, sunlight from evening's ocean like copper. Your thought burnishes bumpy feeling as words splash and spin—the Indian Ocean's in mind as repeating whitecaps and nosediving waves.

17.

We survey the stretched ocean from our blue apartment, and you say, 'only three more days'—back where childhood played out with long burrows and sandy forts. To watch the sky's swallowing gape; to touch a body in teeming, irascible radiance and know flesh as a lugging tide; to pocket shells and opalescent stones—the place would yet write 'belonging' on cracked paving and 'home' on lumpy sidewalks. You say, 'It's inimitable,' marvelling at widening space, even as the apartment's walls close like a tunnel scratched from sand and a girl laughs at the sea running to kiss her toes.

//

'Love', you say, as if the word belongs to us. Your abstractions rain on our bed as a thunderstorm pelts hail. I don't respond, wanting the sour smell of beach sand and the feints of mottled blue swimmer crabs—as if they might mend fractured feeling. Later, as we swim, you kick sideways, following the current, and loss's colours fall from the sky. Rain is a shower of names; as if old affections are painted in purple; as if the water bobs with intimations of the drowned.

18.

We've followed the ocean's old trade routes to islands and waterways; abundances of fruit and market squares; crowded cities and divergent byways. We pause on this coastline where slave ships once harboured and religions collided. The high tide fractures. A bell sounds and a woman begins to sing. 'Though cruel, it was often excruciatingly beautiful,' you say, shrugging, looking away—as if tyrannies have passed. We find a stall selling cold drinks and sit opposite one another, reading separately. The song crests again, with oceanic rhythms. Your book's forgotten on the table as centuries gather in the extended tune, its beauty like an elaborate sword.

19.

Cliffs drop rock slivers, and their splash is time's movement. The ocean trembles in swathes, tugging us, shifting acres of water. You question what holds, asking if we'll come again to this whitewashed village and port. The sea knocks against limestone. A tall woman walks with a baby in a pram. Caves hide shifting ideas of darkness, amplifying the ocean. We buy heads of garlic and aubergines from the market. The tall woman is there again, handling fruit as her baby squalls. Later, we make love. 'The human footprint is vanishing,' you tell me, 'and there's no way back.' In our window, sunset bloodies the water.

20.

The ocean's slow heave nurses our sleep, as if blood is nourished by the water's weight and listening hears no raiders. We drift and are taken in a gyre's hypnosis. The morning's littoral bubbles and settles and boats ply oars where the horizon's distance inches forever. Now, in bed, discussing the day, we sense a convulsion. Our clockface runs with trickles of water and windows dissolve into ragged spume. We're thrown together and pushed apart as words become like tangled seaweed. Though we'd rise, our bodies are sand.

21.

Our muscles contain the walk from the ferry like lengths of sunshine. Margaritas climb in our blood. We dive into the scrawling surf, struck by wind and jostled by water, entering again the site of language in the sudden carriage of turbulence. It intimates what we've never said as we straddle the sea floor that falls away, becoming again the incorrigible child—adrift in feeling and bumped by words.

PACIFIC
a prose poem archipelago
Paul Munden

*'Most people live on a lonely island,
Lost in the middle of a foggy sea.'*

—Rodgers & Hammerstein, 'Bali Ha'i',
   South Pacific

*'They are carried up to the heaven, and down
again to the deep: their soul melteth away
because of the trouble.'*

—Psalm 107

Geography 79
Cannery Row 80
Sweet Thursday 81
Mar Pacifico 82
Sex on the Beach 83
Vertigo 84
Pearl Harbour 85
The Old Iguana 86
Mare Clausum 87
Galápagos 88
Lonesome George 89
Blue-footed booby 90
Sharks 91
Rise and fall 92
Message in a bottle 93
∞ 94
Challenger Deep 95
Easter Day 96
Heron Island 97
Ocean swim 98
Albatross 99

In **Geography**, Mr Birmingham had us colouring around the oceanic rim. We didn't know why. But since colour can be sound, I listened—as I moved my crayons on the page—to rock music playing from the pools and crevices along the shore. In the central void, I sketched in dolphins to add a click track, and whales for the deep harmonic slides. Instrumental and then vocal surf would soon be all the rage, with enough spring reverb to make three-metre waves. Studios began to dot the Californian coast. The Beach Boys' named theirs Brother. In POP, Santa Monica, we followed Professor Lidenbrook's *Return to the Centre of the Earth* from an alternative angle, thrilling to every synthesised blast of volcanic pipes.

If I had to locate the moment it all went wrong, it was *My Beautiful Dark Twisted Fantasy* erupting from Island Sound, Honolulu. For weeks, ash fell on our ears instead of rain. I finally understood Mr Birmingham's ennui.

It's through Mack and Doc's eyes that I get my first glimpse, as they stroll down Ocean View Avenue in Monterey. **Cannery Row**, *a poem, a stink, a grating noise, a quality of light, a tone, a habit, a nostalgia, a dream...* Billy and I stepped into the picture, similarly skint, but we pushed the boat out with Dirty Harry burgers in Clint's restaurant in Carmel, The Hog's Breath Inn, before camping within a cluster of bushes on the beach, nothing over our heads but the stars. In the morning, the sea's blue sparkle was limitless as the future.

Part of me is still adrift there, listening to the ocean crash, that month before Billy and his motorbike hit the tree and his mind turned, like the tide, the sparkle gone from his eyes.

I stare out to sea, waiting.

Years later I read the sequel, **Sweet Thursday**. Hell did we
need it after so many lousy Wednesdays, which nobody
had the heart to write up. Doc had come home after the
War, depressed, and the boys decided to find him a wife.
They should have realised he was already married to
the ocean. They should have realised the future is a pipe
dream, out of reach.

Our Father who art in nature... forgive us our
well-meaning plans that go so catastrophically wrong.
Forgive us all our *bitter*sweet repetitive mistakes, our
wild-child spirit.

Having rounded Cape Horn to the west, the early explorers found an ocean of relative calm: **Mar Pacífico**, the raging sea now pacified, a baby with a comforter clamped like a dummy teat between the gums.

The binky falls, and the baby's raging anxiety resumes, the lull blown away by savage winds, waves thirty feet high.

Later explorers would find a vortex of trash, the Great Pacific Garbage Patch of toys thrown out of humanity's pram.

People warn you about the terrible twos, when the rage can really run amok, just as they do about those older relatives further south, the roaring forties and furious fifties.

The screaming sixties still carry a strangely mythical allure.

When the waitress asks if **Sex on the Beach** is for us, the whole restaurant tunes in, faces turning like searchlights on our table. We look each other in the eye, and smile, thinking of Deborah Kerr and Burt Lancaster frolicking in the waves. There's a little reluctance as we shake our heads. Next time, we're at a table a few feet closer to the door when the highball glass once more comes winking in our direction, its rainbow of cranberry, orange and peach shot through with vodka and ice. There's an erotic rush, *From Here to Eternity*—and beyond, waves breaking over us. In littoral translation, Halona Beach Cove becomes Whitecap Bay for Johnny Depp and Penélope Cruz *On Stranger Tides*. At Halona Point, waves have undercut the ancient lava tubes to form a blowhole that pumps orgasmic spray into the air, geology mimicking the whales offshore, humpbacks whose attention is now similarly aroused. We're all at sea, the current treacherous. The waitress shrugs.

Each morning I'm greeted by the extinct volcano at the east of the island, as I step onto the perilous twenty-seventh floor balcony with only just space for a single chair. Coffee and **vertigo**. Somewhere down there in the shallows are crabs, still flirting with the idea of life on land. I can't at first think what I'm to do here without you.

I hunt for whales with my camera, then the locations for *Jurassic Park*. At Mānoa Falls, I wonder where it is now—the water I saw drop from the big screen skyline on its first release. A dragonfly lifts like a miniature helicopter.

It's late afternoon when I find the Nu'uanu Pali, and learn how you become King by sending 400 men over the cliff to their deaths.

The official evening welcome is a *lū'au,* a pig roasted in the ground with hot rocks until the flesh is ready to be shaken from the bones.

Our host provides a commentary to the feast before bursting into song:

Are you lonesome tonight? Do you miss me tonight? Are you sorry we drifted apart?

In **Pearl Harbour**, a floating memorial straddles the sunken wreckage of the USS Arizona, a single gun turret barbette just visible above the waterline. Black tears still rise from the fractured oil tanks, and I start to believe I can hear a melody in the wind, *a walk down Lonely Street / To Heartbreak Hotel*, Presley's voice, fresh from the army, helping to raise the necessary dollars to honour the dead. I read the one thousand, one hundred and seventy-seven names of the lost. Others' ashes are scattered into the air above the watery grave, even as we add the fine grains of our own losses to the airborne melody. Photos show Presley collecting ever more leis around his neck, loops of kika blossoms, jasmine, orchids …

Every welcome is also a farewell—*you will be lonely / You'll be so lonely, you could die.*

When Mathew Peckinpah joins the Marines, his father, '**The Old Iguana**', writes him a salutary letter:

... 'to do your best you must *learn to read* and *understand what you read* ... and listen—I repeat, listen... You are part of a team and *the team comes first—not you*... When you make a mistake, do something dumb—make a jackass out of yourself—Stop! And I really mean stop berating yourself, or turning it on others. Think it over—write it down. Repeat: Write it down, then remember what caused the problem, how you can fix it and why it won't happen again. Chances are it will, many times. Each time, the lesson will go a little deeper... Most important, don't forget how to laugh—especially at yourself and the devil—not at others' misfortunes... Forget completely any obvious attempts to display superiority to your fellow man. It only demonstrates how little you know. If you have nothing to brag about, don't. If you have something to brag about, it's even more important to keep your *Goddamned mouth shut*... Sometimes homesickness, loneliness, will become almost unbearable... But you've got people who love you—who care about you—and they'll be close... Remember: Boot camp is only the beginning. After that it gets rough...'

The Spanish claimed it a **mare clausum**, but every living thing within these borders was once a migrant: every bird, every seed in beak or faeces. The only jurisdiction was the vagary of the wind. Iguanas arrived on makeshift rafts of vegetation thrown together by a storm, but they soon went native, slivers of volcanic rock chiselled from their terrain. Each chip off the old block then went its own way, some land-lubbers, others sea dogs. You could match a tortoise to its island by the taste of its meat, according to Darwin, the gourmet naturalist. A kinder reckoning was by size.

Clausum, closed... and yet in came the felons, in came disease, the full flood of tribulation and non-proprietary grief.

A creep of tortoises gathers to drink, their shells forming a **Galápagos** archipelago in the swamp: stepping stones across the water; stepping stones—like the islands to which they gave their name—from the future to the past.

Out on dry land, humping, the giant reptiles look dreadfully earnest, awkwardly ill-suited to the task. Perhaps we would look ungainly too, if we were to get it together on this Nature Cruise of the Century. Here we are with our Beagle eyes and metaphorical rats and goats, agents of disruption. It's only a matter of time before an * appears beside certain names, as prelude to their imminent demise. In your spangled, sequined dress you look particularly vulnerable as we make a slow dance around the promenade deck, sharing our silent thoughts.

No man is an island, entire of itself ... never send to know for whom the bell tolls; it tolls for thee.

Lonesome George, you weren't the oldest (that was Jonathan, an ocean apart), just the last man standing of the Pinta Island breed. In your eighties, they were still bringing you prospective mates of close species. You kept in training, gave it your all. *Citius, altius, fortius.* The 2012 games were a mere month away and you'd notched up a remarkable personal best when suddenly your competitive days were at an end.
Plus solitarius.

You're such a **blue-footed booby**. You're always preaching about serial monogamy, but you're plainly an opportunistic breeder, a sexual predator, making catcalls and wolf-whistles at anything attractive flying past. There's no hiding that bigamous streak as you strut your stuff, *one for the money, two for the show*, staring each potential conquest square in the face. Once your bright colour told the girls you were fit, with your *blue, blue suede shoes, oh baby*. Now your blues are fading, and their attention is turning to the younger males.

You plunge a hundred feet like a knife into water, hunting sardines, anchovies, mackerel, squid. When your multiple wives take their turn, you get extra time off.

You take stock of the shit-circled nest: only the larger eggs will do. Your children are as callous, thinking nothing of the siblicide to which you turn a blind eye.

basking**sharks**bigeyethresher**sharks**bignose **sharks**blacktipreef**sharks**blue**sharks**bluntnosesixgill **sharks**bonnethead**sharks**broadnosesevengill**sharks**brown cat**sharks**brownsmoothhound**sharks**bullsharkscombtooth dogfish**sharks**commonthresher**sharks**cookiecutter**sharks** copper**sharks**crocodile**sharks**dusky**sharks**filetailcat**sharks** frilled**sharks**galapagos**sharks**goblin**sharks**greathammerhead **sharks**greatwhite**sharks**greyreef**sharks**greysmoothhound **sharks**horn**sharks**lemon**sharks**leopard**sharks**lollipopcat **sharks**longnosecat**sharks**magamouth**sharks**oceanicwhite tip**sharks**Pacificangle**sharks**Pacificsleeper**sharks**pelagic thresher**sharks**pepperedcat**sharks**pigmy**sharks**prickly **sharks**raggedtooth**sharks**salmon**sharks**sandbar**sharks** scallopedbonnethead**sharks**scallopedhammerhead**sharks** school**sharks**scoophead**sharks**sicklefinsmoothhound **sharks**smoothhammerhead**sharks**silky**sharks**silver tip**sharks**smalltail**sharks**smallspottedcat**sharks**smooth hound**sharks**soupfin**sharks**spinydogfish**sharks**shortfin mako**sharks**swell**sharks**tawnynurse**sharks**tiger**sharks** whale**sharks**whitenose**sharks**whitetipreef**sharks**

The islands rise and fall like recalcitrant animatronics. Gone are the earliest models, submerged, as new versions test the water. They too will be replaced, as they move away from the mantle plume, the volcanic hotspot.

Each attempt is both a creative spurt and a piece of wreckage, *a whole new start and a different kind of failure*, moving across the oceanic page, south-east, a couple of inches a year, like markers on the map of a slow campaign.

All around, waves find new ways to say the same thing over and over again, their niggling comments repeated *ad nauseam*. It's a war of attrition, without imaginable end.

I wander the beach, gleaning stories from the finely ground bones and shells, but finding no solace. The Desert Island jukebox in my head kicks in with *more loneliness than any man could bear*. With every tide, words and phrases reach me from other oceans, where 'waves freeze' and scientists wear 'fur-lined boots'. Some read like miniature poems, bereft of their line breaks. There are secrets, kept from husband or wife, shared with the anonymity of the sea. A condom washed up on the sand still carries its coded, glutinous dregs. Everything reeks of sex and death. Once, a **message in a bottle** rolled in amongst the flotsam and jetsam, its desperation still thriving on the meagre supply of air. Then another, and another... *Seems I'm not alone at being alone.*

∞ all that's visible is water and more unfathomable water, a blur, nothing so well-defined as the doldrums to hold onto, and yet somewhere out here is *the oceanic pole of inaccessibility*, beguilingly precise, but forever out of reach ~ somewhere here too is the place where time is at its most elusive, a conceptual line where future and past can converge ≈ the current takes us in perpetual circles ~ we're migrants following a möbius strip, desperate for a footing in the present ≈ grey-black water hangs above us, a lugubrious pall ≈ where there should be a horizon, there's simply water folding into the air, folding into infinity's loop ~ no sun, no stars ~ the gps went awol many invisible moons ago, leaving us to take our bearings from pure limbo ≈ an eternity of water, claustrophobic as the smallest room ∞

On **Heron Island**, we walk across the reef flat, or swim over it at high tide. Sharks circle us—reef sharks, surely, all harmless, though they look bigger than me, bigger each time they revolve into view. You always joked about that menacing theme of alternating notes as the limit of your prowess on the sax. Entranced, I stay too long in the water, and the skin on my shoulders begins to burn. At sunset, a bride and groom are framed by the sad Casuarina trees, a pair of white-bellied sea eagles high overhead. You seemed troubled, burdened with things you knew would be hard to say.

I woke you early, to watch the green turtles haul themselves ashore to lay their eggs. I wondered if I could ever bear to come back, and see the hatchlings run the gauntlet of the beach, witness some being picked off by gulls before they even reached the water. Now that you're gone, I know the answer even less.

The stepping stones take you back to childhood, each step a further intimation of mortality.

Out here the steps are far apart, and yet you crossed them with alarming speed.

No mountain on earth goes up as far as **Challenger Deep** goes down within the Mariana Trench. Thirty-five thousand feet and more, still only just enough for my thoughts to find a home —a watery place *too deep for tears*.

It looms, then vanishes, becomes myth: the 'navel of the world'. Perhaps it was another of the Unfortunate Islands, another Roca Catedral, known only to the birds. It's **Easter Day** when it finally crystallizes on the map, unmistakable with its line of gargantuan torsos, half buried, or perhaps half risen from the body of the island, like gods of pure volcanic ash.

In the days after you die, I find myself at an Easter service, despite losing my religion. I think how, if I were to construct one, it would be made of our favourite things.

Waves break over my newly formed island, as I watch the flocks of birds rehearse their tilting choreography.

All around the cathedral the saints and apostles, carved by the wind, *look down* as if they know the very song that surges in my mind:

Though her words are simple and few / 'Listen, listen', she's calling to you.

'Feed the birds, tuppence a bag, tuppence, tuppence, tuppence a bag.'

As the sun comes up, a whole crowd takes to the water for their daily **ocean swim** along Australia's east coast. Moving parallel to the shore, they have the whole Pacific Rim in their sights. The Ring of Fire is further out: there's no danger of falling in.

A poet is (of course) to blame for the craze, Byron setting out across the Hellespont, his club foot an insufficient impediment to his ambition. *Roll on, thou deep and dark blue ocean—roll!* And the swimmers roll with it, religiously, each day.

For a few weekends you joined them, completing at least one small stretch of the coast, a stretch I will forever hold dear.

There is rapture on the lonely shore.

From Doubtful Sound we journeyed into the Tasman sea, where once again the captain cut the engine, and pointed to the sky. He had an eye for it—the smallest of crosshairs tracking across cloud. As it circled lower, the phenomenal span of the **albatross** became apparent, and *silence sank like music on my heart*. How many years since it touched land, I wondered, even as I pondered how an ancient Rime had travelled to reach me, here, in the remotest place I'd ever been. The bird made no wingbeat, it was the centre of the calm that held us in thrall. We watched as it glided slowly away, fearful of the moment we knew would come, the engine once more throttling into its parallel life.

NOTES TO THE POEMS

1. Island Sound Studios was formerly Avex Honolulu Studios, where Kanye West recorded *My Beautiful Dark Twisted Fantasy* (2010).
2. John Steinbeck, *Cannery Row* (1945).
3. John Steinbeck, *Sweet Thursday* (1954).
4. Ferdinand Magellan coined the name *Mar Pacifico* (peaceful sea) in 1521.
5. From *Here to Eternity*, dir. Zinnemann (1930); *Pirates of the Caribbean: On Stranger Tides*, dir. Marshall (2011). Halona Beach Cove, aka Cockroach Cove, is on the Hawaiian island of Oahu.
6. Elvis Presley, 'Are You Lonesome Tonight?' (1960).
7. Elvis Presley, 'Heartbreak Hotel' (1956). Presley's USS Arizona Benefit Concert was staged at the Bloch Arena, 25 March 1961 (National Medal of Honor Day).
8. Sam Peckinpah's son Mathew, who struggled with dyslexia, joined the Marine Corps in 1980, four years before his father's death.
9. Spain, during the fifteenth and sixteenth centuries, considered the Pacific Ocean to be a *mare clausum*, a sea closed to other naval powers.
10. Kurt Vonnegut, *Galápagos* (1985); John Donne, 'No Man is an Island' (1624).
12. Elvis Presley, 'Blue Suede Shoes' (1956)
13. A fairly comprehensive list of sharks inhabiting the Pacific.
14. TS Eliot, 'East Coker' from *Four Quartets* (1943).
15. The Police, 'Message in a Bottle' (1979).
16. The Oceanic Pole of inaccessibility, between Chile and New Zealand, is the farthest point from any landmass on Earth (1,670 miles). The International Date line (approximately 180° longitude) divides one calendar day from the next.
18. The nearest islands to Challenger Deep are Fais (287km southwest) and Guam (304km northeast).
19. 'Feed the Birds' from *Mary Poppins*, dir. Stevenson (1964). Philip Larkin, 'Water' (1954): 'If I were called in / To construct a religion / I should make use of water.' Jacob Roggeveen coined the name Easter Island having come across the island on Easter Day, 1722.
20. Lord Byron, 'Childe Harold's Pilgrimage' (1812–18); Johnny Cash, 'Ring of Fire' (1963). Byron crossed the Hellespont on 3 May 1810.
21. Samuel Taylor Coleridge, 'Rime of the Ancient Mariner' (1798).

THE SOUTHERN OCEAN
Jen Webb

'How inappropriate to call this planet Earth, when it is clearly Ocean'
—Arthur C Clarke, in *Nature*, 8 March 1990

'The sea is as near as we come to another world'
—Anne Stevenson, 'North Sea Off Carnoustie'

1. Antarctic Convergence   105
Latitude: between -60° and -45°; Longitude: variable

2. Cape of Good Hope   106
-34.3548306; 18.469830555555554

3. The Roaring Forties, Possession Island   107
-46.4166667; 51.98305555555556

4. The Furious Fifties, Heard Island   108
-53.0830706; 73.5325035

5. Cape Leeuwin   109
-34.3711639; 115.134833333333

6. North Cape, Motu Ihupuku   110
-52.5374548; 169.1783149

7. Sandy Point   111
-46.4118465; 168.3470632

8. Mid ocean, no resolved address   112
-60.52021475816397; 179.21873882738328

9. Antarctica, no resolved address   113
-78.93981625096974; -39.99298095703125

10. Mawson's hut, Cape Denison   114
-67.0088; 142.6609

11. McMurdo Station   115
-77.846323, 166.668235

12. 3,800 feet deep, no resolved address   116
-77.47982610478525; 179.51368650632588

13. Cape Flying Fish   117
-72.8333333; -107.54999972222222

14. Thwaites Ice Tongue				118
-75.3; -106.45

15. Peter Island				119
-68.85; -90.58333333333333

16. Bellingshausen Sea, no resolved address				120
-67.38584650230459; -78.27589925130206

17. Graham Land				121
-66.1536138; -63.2201954

18. South Shetland Islands				122
-62.6079191; -60.65962

19. Cape Disappointment				123
-54.882226053138226; -36.12080709756084

20. Bouvet Island				124
-54.42; 03.36

21. Gqeberha, Algoa Bay				125
-33.9580556; 25.6

1. ANTARCTIC CONVERGENCE

Latitude: between -60° and -45°; Longitude: variable

The world is curling around itself, a child self-soothing in a dark night. The gyro at its heart pauses, swivels, resets, and we stagger a little as the tremble reaches the surface. Water flowing fast, keeping the world afloat. If architecture begins with a grave in the forest, if art begins with a single fingertip in ochre, then surely we too can pretend that everything is starting anew?

2. CAPE OF GOOD HOPE

-34.3548306; 18.469830555555554

My lover is a seagull. Stealing my chips, screaming in my sleep.

My lover sets out in early morning, alpenstock and tam o' shanter, earbuds fully charged. And yes the lagoon is in flood but he remembers fording it as a boy, unharmed. He takes a swig from his hip flask, dips his toes into raging seas.

My lover is a seal. Pressed against the tide on a rock off Robben Island. His satin coat. His impervious gaze. The distance.

My lover is the sea, reaching out fine fingers to caress my legs. Hot passion against night-time sand. Carrying me off in powerful rips to the zone of no way back.

My lover is the sky, looking down as I float face up in the sea.

3. THE ROARING FORTIES, POSSESSION ISLAND

-46.4166667; 51.98305555555556

The storm came in like a spell murmuring bad weather
into my ear, and kept coming, spilling over the mouth
of the hull, salt water, rainwater, hermit crabs and kelp.
You reached for the mop and brushed at the mess. Water
kept rising and the ship's cat spidered around its margins,
and thunder came in hard, shaking the sails, tracer shells
bursting the portholes, waves wagging their fingers at us,
reminders of all we'd fail to do.

4. THE FURIOUS FIFTIES, HEARD ISLAND

-53.0830706; 73.5325035

No you can't make landfall, not on this land where dead volcano meets howling gale, though if you could, you would shelter in the caldera and pretend you don't have weeks yet to fight your way further west, against the polar current, flying in the teeth of the wind. It's not that you fear the country or the sea. It's not that you fear those other selves. But you can't deny, not even in the silence of your watch, that they would throw you overboard to save themselves. Can you trust your fellow sailors? Trust those you love? You nod, thoughtfully, and check the sextant.

5. CAPE LEEUWIN

-34.3711639; 115.13483333333333

Here in quiet lands, you wake in the wrong bed after nights of deadman sleep. Walk in the dawn across wet sand, watched by possums and a cautious cat, stretch like the trees toward the sky. In the distance, rumble of ocean. You have escaped the southern gales, but albatross, orca, ice tongue—they are waiting for you further south, waiting for you and your gaiters and gloves, your beacons and your batteries. Is this really who you want to be?

6. NORTH CAPE, MOTU IHUPUKU

-52.5374548; 169.1783149

Now we start our training for the true south: taking cold baths, doing laps in winter, sleeping sans sheets. My skin blistered, yours grew chapped. We are not scientists who go all the way—fur-lined boots, snow glasses, safety gear. We pick a path between the rocks to the southern beach, sans anorak, sans boots. Our skin blossoms under the gale, glows where spray traces salty fingers across us. This is nearly ice; this is nearly the south of the south; this is where the scant stories begin.

7. SANDY POINT

-46.4118465; 168.3470632

The weather is late winter, the latitude as far south as a person can be without being on Antarctica. My sister is there after waving us off to the cold deep. She is making pictures of whatever she can see. She stands at the end of the island, watching grey water and black water and grey sky construct a complex weave she will render in graphite and washed ink wash. The ocean rackets around the shores, living up to the stories sailors relate. Rocks lie calm as seals in foaming shallows, or interrupt the urgent rush of waves, and the spray flies up, turns into lace. She watches, wondering what new thing she might make.

8. MID OCEAN, NO RESOLVED ADDRESS

-60.52021475816397; 179.21873882738328

Seventeen weeks at sea and what a sea. We scoot along on the surface of the deepest currents known; fast water below us, swift winds above. And yes icebergs, as they'd promised, so we take turns on deck, one sleeping, the other leaning out above the abyss to haul the boat around another berg. *So far so good* you say on waking each dawn and I essay a wave—*meh*—and stumble down to bed. Middays we share a beer and try to raise Australia on the phone but no good so far, no good. We are cast on our own resources, on the songs of whales, the purrs and trills of leopard seals. *Could be worse,* you say. Could be so much worse.

9. ANTARCTICA, NO RESOLVED ADDRESS

-78.93981625096974; -39.99298095703125

At this temperature waves freeze and only muscle-bound dolphins keep moving, one eye menacing our stalled boat where we hover between the air and the sea. They circle in the fragments of free water, mocking. *You said they were friendly,* comes a cracked voice, and we shrug, trying to seem sanguine, knowing we are out of our depth. *You have to admit it's gorgeous,* says someone else, and we turn, a choreography of fret, and stare at the white on blue on white, the chitter of sunbeams across the ice, the rafts of penguins circling us, laughing.

10. MAWSON'S HUT, CAPE DENISON

-67.0088; 142.6609

Snow metres deep. Snow spilling through the windows. History spilling through the windows. Next door there's a gift shop selling narwhals and polar bears in miniature. Polar bears? *Go figure*, says the salesman, shrugging. Orcas and penguins crowd around the window display, surprised. *It's all one ocean, really*, says the salesman, and we shake our heads. *No*, we say. *No way.*

11. MCMURDO STATION

-77.846323, 166.668235

We dip toe into water and our white skin turns red. Wind chill is worse so we dive in, submerging, forgetting how to breathe. Penguins dive in after us, waving as they fly pass, and we twist in the ice, heading back toward the sky. You reach the surface first and the scientists haul you up and into furs, take your temperature, monitor the change. I remain adrift, captured by the fall of light on ice, how saltwater turns silver, how antiquity inscribes itself along the reef. Till someone's hand snatches me, someone is mouth to mouth pumping heat into my bones. The shore shifts against the anchor ice; everything goes on as before.

12. 3,800 FEET DEEP, NO RESOLVED ADDRESS

-77.47982610478525; 179.51368650632588

Once in a good year the sun threads a line to deep water, and the stars who live in the caverns of the sea perk up. *Strawberry feather stars, to be precise,* says the scientist. *Pure eldritch horror* says the journalist, then laughs, ever so slightly off edge. Strange beings flutter like burlesque dancers, tucking their stalk between the folds and fronds of their flesh, stretching their feathers. You paddle your coracle between the ice shelves, determined to make first contact. Imagining what you might say.

13. CAPE FLYING FISH

-72.8333333; -107.54999972222222

The phone pings, and it's Qantas, offering me an upgrade on my next flight though I'm not flying anywhere just now. We are huddled in our fur-lined tent, waiting for the weather to turn. The sea has gone from great pale rollers to deepthroat crunching of ice floes assaulting the shore. Four of us crammed in here; one too many for the design specifications but no one's volunteering to do a Captain Oates. All you wanted was a few weeks alone with me; all they wanted was the chance to measure the snow; all I wanted was one day at the Cape, just me and the ocean and the way the sun falls, here at the very bottom of the world.

14. THWAITES ICE TONGUE

-75.3; -106.45

Lighting a fire in an earnest attempt to get the team back home, because no one else understands ice. I rely on fleecy boots. You opt for the skidoo. Others are committed to trudging.

Ships rust in fields of anchor ice, the boat failed to reach the fuel tanks, stokers are shovelling socks and sandwiches into the flames but the fleet is going nowhere fast.

Icebergs stretch and yawn, and roll over in bed. Boats scrabble for the surface; we run for higher ground.

15. PETER ISLAND

-68.85; -90.58333333333333

The ocean is eating us, one by one. We do all we can to avoid its grasp, ignoring strange creatures that dwell beneath the anchor ice, ignoring the currents of the convergence. Yesterday we sailed across four degrees, across angry ice through the screaming sixties, our long adventure. When I leapt to shore the ice sent me slipperysliding into the sea. A whale on the edge of the bay gazed with what I read as compassion. Five penguins clustered on the shore, watching with interest. Someone threw me a raft, someone threw me a rope, you waded in waist deep and pulled me free.

16. BELLINGSHAUSEN SEA, NO RESOLVED ADDRESS

-67.38584650230459; -78.27589925130206

The plane creaks at every joint then finds its light and rackets up to fifteen thousand feet, higher than the towers of clouds. Flight without feathers: an everyday miracle. It crests cloud mountain then skis down for a closer look at the world, looking for us. Looking at the seals who roll themselves off the ice floes and into ice water when they hear its engines; at the sleepy whiteness of snow; at the tent that sits bright blue against the snow, and the man outside it, bright yellow in hi-vis, who is waving both tiny arms, ready to catch the bag full of just-add-water soup the plane will drop, of strike-anywhere matches that will light the tiny stove, the stove that once lit will heat the water. Another everyday miracle. Another few days on shore.

17. GRAHAM LAND

-66.1536138; -63.2201954

I don't want to talk about climate change, but look, shit is coming down. Moths appear, fluttering, in Antarctica. They have forgotten how cold feels, forgotten their hunger for jumpers and socks.

An iceberg turned turtle a week ago and the TikTok generation are posting videos of themselves dancing on its dark blue folds. You spent three hours stretched out on the same ice, photographing its change. Meantime I made a bowl of Insta-soup and sent pictures to my Super group.

I am watching the sun that seems just a little too close. I am listening to how ice groans as it faces a future of salt.

18. SOUTH SHETLAND ISLANDS

-62.6079191; -60.65962

Boats are crossing. Not all make safe landfall. You are up in the crow's nest, freezing your arse off, taking notes. Icebergs. High winds. High seas. Once you blamed an orca but you were bored that hour. You tighten the drawstring on your snowsuit. Fingertips turning blue. Penguins look at you, curiously, and there's still no word from home, and nothing to take to bed but the last drop of Scotch.

19. CAPE DISAPPOINTMENT

-54.882226053138226; -36.12080709756084

We row row row the boat but the waves are swelling and the rip tide running and finally you ship the oars and let the water sweep us out into the bay, announcing that once the tide turns it will propel us back to the lagoon. I wonder about your wisdom when a three-metre shark swims speculatively alongside but it loses interest before you do and heads off on fish business. No one knows we're out here. No one is checking the time, calling my number, listening to the ring-ring, ring-ring until it turns to voicemail. We are now at the mouth of the bay and waves are smashing against the reef and the tide hasn't turned. You close your eyes, hum gently to yourself, listen to the sounds of the sea.

20. BOUVET ISLAND

-54.42; 03.36

Inside the tent the lights are muted blue, outside a rare falling star splashes light like sun, and the waves and trees duck below their shadows while a blurred half moon hangs overhead, watching. I am watching too, in the neither here nor there, neither grounded nor in flight. We are drifting toward the bardo, the not-here space where those who are lost find they can find themselves on this unmapped terrain. It's how timezones align themselves to each other, how multiworlds hold hands briefly, and we slide between them, leaving fractal shadows that fall like light where no light falls.

21. GQEBERHA, ALGOA BAY

-33.9580556; 25.6

South is where we started, and where we'll end. Deep channels run east northeast, like the whales do, and we run with them, murmuring alerts when mechanical growl makes its way through the waves. Fishing boats are armed and on patrol, heading south, so the whales head west and we turn too, lean back against the currents and drift, as sea creatures do, ice against our backs, sun on our faces, alone but for sailors who lean out from the crow's nest, hoping for just one glimpse.

INDIVIDUAL POETS' STATEMENTS

CASSANDRA ATHERTON

This sequence of prose poems is written in response to Matthew Olzmann's 'For a Recently Discovered Shipwreck at the Bottom of Lake Michigan'.[1] It begins:

> 4/2/2010
> Dear Shipwreck,
> Even though you're over a century old, they say that everything inside you is still intact, Even the crew? Must be lonely. I'll write again.

In the eight prose poems that form a chain of unanswered missives, the narrator reveals the shipwreck is *The L.R. Doty*, a wooden steamship that sank in a storm in 1898. In these poetic apostrophes, the shipwreck is addressed as both the personification of the narrator's existential crisis and a 'Metaphor for God'. Indeed, Emilia Phillips argues, in this poem, 'The poet becomes both the letter writer and the ship, the voice and the silence'.[2] There are some wonderfully neo-surreal and parodic moments when the narrator is angered by the shipwreck's lack of response:

> 6/29/2010
> Dear Mister-Too-Good-To-Write-Anyone-Back,
> Fuck you, man. I don't care if you didn't like that poem. That's no
> excuse for ignoring my letters. I will say this real slowly

---

[1] Olzmann, M (2010) 'For a Recently Discovered Shipwreck at the Bottom of Lake Michigan', *On Earth As It Is*, 48. https://digitalcommons.butler.edu/onearth/48.
[2] Phillips, E (n.d.) 'The Surface Is Really the Sky: A review of Matthew Olzmann's *MEZZANINES* (Alice James Books, 2013)'. http://32poems.com/prose/prose-feature-omnibus-review-matthew-olzmann-marcus-wicker-prose-editor-emilia-phillips/.

for you:
Write. Me. Back. You. Dick.

Today, the wreck of *The L.R. Doty* remains upright at the bottom of the lake. Deep divers found there is still corn in the ship's hold and believe it's likely the crew's bodies are preserved in the boiler room. This reminded me of the most famous shipwreck, which lies 3.8 kilometers below sea level in the North Atlantic Ocean—*RMS Titanic*. I wanted to write an apostrophe in the form of epistolic prose poems to this shipwreck to explore the marine sublime and its connection to desire, intimacy and mortality.

The hubristic narrative of the *Titanic* is well rehearsed: on 10 April 1912, *RMS Titanic* left Southampton on her maiden voyage to New York, via Cherbourg, France and Queenstown, Ireland. Touted as 'unsinkable', just before midnight on 14 April the ship hit an iceberg, broke in two, and foundered two hours and forty minutes later. 1,517 people died. Perhaps unsurprisingly, first class passengers had the highest survival rate at 62 percent, followed by second class at 41 percent, and third class at 25 percent. As Nashwa Khan points out, 'The death rate for all individuals on the *Titanic* decreased as socioeconomic states and cabin class increased'.[3]

I have had a macabre fascination with the *Titanic* since Robert Ballard found the wreck in 1985. I wrote my Honours thesis on Captain Lord of the *Californian* who was somewhere between five and twenty miles away and the only ship who could have reached the *Titanic* before she sank, and I have seen artefacts salvaged (or stolen)

---

[3] Khan, N (2016) 'What the Titanic Reveals About Class and Life Expectancy', *JSTOR Daily*, Business and Economics, 2 June. https://daily.jstor.org/what-the-titanic-reveals-about-class-and-life-expectancy/.

from the wreck in Las Vegas (this exhibition is due to open in Melbourne on my birthday this year!). My first name is also entwined with expressions of tragedy and discussions of the *Titanic*, for example:

> As she steamed at high speed through the dark of night her captain ignored the Cassandra-like warnings that icebergs lurked nearby, and through hubris the ship collided with one.[4]

My prose poetry sequence explores the marine sublime and its connection to desire. It also charts a (w)reckless response to the discovery of a genetic mutation in my DNA, twinned with a fascination in the *Titanic* shipwreck. My prose poems reference Baudelaire's 'Man and the Sea' from *Les fleurs du mal* (1857) and Alain Corbin's *The Lure of the Sea: The discovery of the seaside in the western world 1750–1840* (1988). As Natalie Deam argues, 'Rather than losing the poet within the sublime marine depths, Baudelaire's analogies flatter the poet by expanding his soaring ideals and tortured soul to encompass oceanic infinitudes of space and time'.[5] In *The Lure of the Sea*, a history of French oceans, Corbin argues:

> Towards the end of the eighteenth century, at the time when Cook and Bougainville were making their travels, the ocean would call forth the image of a 'vast expanse' that was indifferent to human time, like the desert; a place of sublime vacuity whose imagined depth was modelled on the very perpendicular sides of the mountains that often bordered it.[6]

I saw myself in the first footage of the *Titanic*'s bow as it

---

[4] Schlenoff, DC (2012) 'Titanic: Resonance and Reality', *Scientific American*, 4 April. https://www.scientificamerican.com/article/titanic-resonance-reality/.
[5] Deam, N (2019) 'The Great Melancholy Mother: Michelet's evolutionary ocean in the sea', in *The Aesthetics of the Undersea*, edited by M Cohen and K Quigley, London and New York: Routledge, 83–96.
[6] Corbin, A (1988) *The Lure of the Sea*, London: Penguin, 127.

slowly came into focus—upright on the ocean floor—73 years after its sinking. The prose poems in my 'Dear Shipwreck' sequence respond to an extension of the marine sublime in what I term the *Titanic* sublime—or the ineffability of the decayed wreck as she sits on the abyssal plain, slowly being devoured by metal-eating bacteria.

Finally, it is true that I have a tiny piece of coal from the *Titanic*'s bunker. I was also given a *Titanic* ice cube tray, a tiny replica of the *Titanic* for the bath and I have cooked dishes from the *Titanic*'s menus. I'm not a fan of the James Cameron film; I much prefer *A Night to Remember* (1958).

OZ HARDWICK

I have only ever visited the Arctic Circle once—a 60th birthday treat, indulging my apparently peculiar attraction to the cold—but in a way I have always thought that I grew up in its silent and unspoken presence.

The last photograph taken of my father shows him holding the Arctic Star, a medal retrospectively instituted in December 2012 and awarded to those in operational service north of the Arctic Circle between 3 September 1939 and 8 May 1945. As then Prime Minister David Cameron said at a Downing Street ceremony which belatedly honoured these veterans,

> It was not just the Arctic conditions, the extraordinary weather; it was also the odds of not coming home at all … It is hard to think of working under such difficult conditions and such appalling odds.[7]

It pains me to quote 'Dave' Cameron with such approbation. My mother once observed that, 'Your great-

---

[7] https://www.gov.uk/government/speeches/transcript-of-arctic-star-medal-presentation-speech.

grandmother would have voted for a pig if it had a blue rosette on it, but she wouldn't have voted for him.' I would remember this when, shortly before her death, the so-called 'Piggate' scandal flooded the news,[8] and again in 2021 when Boris Johnson—the Tweedledee to Cameron's Tweedledum—chose in his address to the Confederation of British Industry, shaken by the ongoing pandemic and starting to feel the disastrous effects of Brexit, to imitate car noises and extol the merits of Peppa Pig World.[9]

As I write, Rishi Sunak, the latest in the line of Johnson's unelected successors, is back-pedalling on environmental commitments in order to ensure that issues such as catastrophic climate change do not 'unnecessarily give people more hassle and more costs in their lives'.[10] That the economic challenges which he allegedly wishes to ameliorate are due in no small part to his laddish predecessors' childish spat which led the UK out of Europe, of course, goes unmentioned. Still, freed from worrisome European governance, it's easier for him to renege on previous solemn commitments. And this is in the year in which we would otherwise be celebrating the half century since the UK joined the Common Market,[11] cementing an alliance which, for many, signalled the incontrovertible end of historic divisions which had previously led to men like my dad fearing for their lives in silent ships at minus thirty degrees.

---

[8] *Call Me Dave* (2015), an unauthorised biography by Michael Ashcroft and Isabel Oakeshott, alleged that Cameron, while an Oxford student, had inserted 'a private part of his anatomy' into a dead pig's mouth during an initiation ceremony for the Piers Gaveston Society.
[9] The embarrassing spectacle may be viewed at https://www.youtube.com/watch?v=dBktY__3Wls.
[10] https://www.theguardian.com/politics/2023/jul/24/rishi-sunak-suggests-delay-or-abandon-green-net-zero-pledges.
[11] The United Kingdom's membership of the European Economic Community came into effect on 1 January 1973.

Recent research suggests that, since 1979, the Arctic has been warming almost four times faster than the rest of the planet.[12] The polar bear has long been the poster beast for environmental catastrophe,[13] while other species native to the region, from orcas to red knots, face increasing threat of extinction in what the World Wildlife Fund refers to as the 'ground zero' of climate change.[14] In the face of this, the ironically-named Lord Frost, former Tory minister and Brexit negotiator, has claimed that we should move away from costly climate change mitigation strategies as, 'At the moment, seven times as many people die from cold as from heat in Britain. Rising temperatures are likely to be beneficial.'[15] Just to clarify: this is *not* satire.

By sheer chance, I'm writing this on the tenth anniversary of Dad's death, hence particularly thinking about that last photo, which is pinned above my desk. For him, the weather could never be warm enough, and in the picture, although it's summer in south-west England, he's wearing a thick cardigan, zipped up to the neck. Although he very rarely spoke about it—barely a handful of brief references in all those years—I've always felt that he carried that Arctic cold in his bones for the rest of his long, quiet life. The elephant in my childhood room was carved out of ice, though that's now melting as we enter

---

[12] Rantanen, M, AY Karpechko and A Lipponen et al. (2022) 'The Arctic Has Warmed Nearly Four Times Faster than the Globe Since 1979', *Communications: Earth and Environment* 3, 168. https://doi.org/10.1038/s43247-022-00498-3.

[13] It should be noted, however, that this adoption is not unproblematic: https://www.theguardian.com/environment/2023/aug/30/why-it-may-be-time-to-stop-using-the-polar-bear-as-a-symbol-of-the-climate-crisis.

[14] https://www.wwf.org.uk/updates/11-arctic-species-affected-climate-change.

[15] https://www.independent.co.uk/news/uk/britain-lord-brexit-government-athens-b2381122.html.

what UN Secretary-General António Guterres recently heralded as the era of 'global boiling'.[16]

Against a mounting catastrophe towards which the UK's increasingly insular and self-absorbed government turns its back, my poems explore the idea of the Arctic, in which my father—an old man, a young man, a dead man—strives silently to embody a selfless, fearful, fragile hope.

PAUL HETHERINGTON

For about twenty-four years, from the age of eight, I lived in Perth, Western Australia, on part of the eastern edge of the Indian Ocean. During that time the ocean fascinated and entranced me. Like so many Western Australians, I swam in it often—not only during extended summers when the beach sand was sometimes so hot it was painful to walk on, but in winter and spring when, as a boy, I attended a surf lifesaving club and from late August onwards regularly battled the swell around the colourful, heaving buoys. Later, when I was a teenager, the beach became a location for night wandering, sometimes with companions, and for swimming under moonlight.

But the ocean was much more than a place to enjoy. As I grew older, I thought of it in many different and divergent ways—as representing vast distances; as the epitome of grandeur and indefinable beauty; as an important boundary, both between peoples and between states of being and understanding; as an enabler of sensuous life; and as a language-shaper and rhythm-giver—something important to an aspiring poet. (And, of course, oceans figure centrally in literature, prompting my allusions to Homer's *Iliad* and Joseph Conrad's work.)

---

[16] https://news.un.org/en/story/2023/07/1139162.

At high school I rather lazily scanned maps and geography texts and learned what the different oceans were—and, broadly speaking, what their relationships to one another were considered to be. Perhaps there was a sense of wanderlust nascent in me at that time. I also began to realise how fragile the Indian Ocean's ecosystems were and how humankind continued to exploit and damage them, often for no good reason. Subsequently, I became aware of the climate emergency and the extremely deleterious effects global warming is having on oceans and ocean life.

This includes damage to all sorts of complex human societies and cultures and their relationships with one another—many of which extend a long way into the past. As Prasannan Parthasarathi and Giorgio Riello aver, 'The Indian Ocean, like the Mediterranean but unlike the Atlantic or Pacific, has a dense history of connections dating back to ancient times.'[17] Such connectedness, and its inexpressibly deep significances, have been attested to by numerous people in a wide variety of ways—and the quotations in this poetry sequence from the anonymous work, the *Periplus Maris Erythraei* (*The Voyage Around the Erythraean Sea*), written around the mid-first-century CE, are designed to emphasise the point.

Indeed, not only am I interested in the way the ocean has enabled trade and cultural exchanges throughout history, I have also become increasingly aware of the Indian Ocean's contemporary geo-political importance. My poems contain important lateral references to what Anne K Bang characterises as:

> a specific discourse [in recent decades] which goes beyond the local and focuses instead on inter-

---

[17] Parthasarathi, P, and G Riello (2014) 'The Indian Ocean in the Long Eighteenth Century', *Eighteenth-Century Studies* 48 (1), 2.

civilizational encounters and the ensuing cultural change. Words like 'hybrid', 'polyphonic', 'cosmopolitan', 'pluralist', 'multi-cultural' can be found ... and reflect the emphasis on *movement* and *exchange* as starting points.[18]

My poems stress ideas of movement, exchange and development, along with the repetitions and reiterations of memory and feeling. As part of this troping, they refer to destructive European colonial ventures in the Indian Ocean, including notions of 'Empire' and warfare. They also explore ideas of connection between individuals with different backgrounds and assumptions, giving emphasis to the ocean's significance in the personal life and relationships of the poems' protagonists, while gesturing toward cultural diversity and the spaces the ocean permits for contemplation and reflection.

More generally, these poems are partly intended as a meditation on how the ocean is at the heart of a great deal of thinking and experience—even though it is sometimes seen to be at the periphery of people's lives. All continents abut the ocean and are at least partly defined by it; all land-dwellers are aware of the importance of the sea. Even for desert societies or for landlocked nation states, the distance from or proximity to the sea is of considerable symbolic, psychological and practical importance.

Finally, notions of the personal, the literary, the social, the political and the historical have so often coalesced for me around images of the ocean. In the littoral, I have so often gathered driftwood, shells or pebbles; and I have frequently stood with waves insistently gathering my feet. The ocean remains an entity to contemplate and

---

[18] Bang, AK (2009) 'Reflections on The History of The Indian Ocean: The sources and their relation to local practices and global connectivities', *Transforming Cultures eJournal* 4 (2), 1-2. http://epress.lib.uts.edu.au/journals/TfC.

ponder. It presents persistent and often inspiring visions of salutary beauty and unresolvable mysteries—some of them so intimate as to crowd the palm of the hand.

PAUL MUNDEN

When making my choice of ocean, I was immediately drawn to the Pacific, having visited not only the bordering Australian and American coasts but also Hawai'i, while a trip to the Galápagos Islands has long been my ambition. Those famous archipelagos came to dominate my thoughts, and suggested a structure for this sequence of poems: an archipelago of erupted musings, shifting across the recurrent page. I also had a new reason to shun the classic rectangular shape of the prose poem, preferring where possible the more ragged 'island' shape afforded by paragraph breaks.

    I had some knowledge of those places I had visited, but the Pacific ocean as a whole was a vast, unknown thing to me, and so—for the first time, in embarking on one of these prose poem sequences—I undertook considerable research. But even as I gained a better understanding, something seemed to tell me that a body of water of such magnitude may always remain beyond the scope of scientific charter, a profound enigma.

    Ever since the *C19* anthology, which explored ekphrasis and intertextuality, I have welcomed a whole range of artistic references into my prose poems, most recently (in 'Sweet') the world of popular song. In this case it's Elvis Presley who presides. But there are also literary works that exert an influence: John Steinbeck's *Cannery Row*, and Kurt Vonnegut's *Galapagos*, two of my favourite novels. And as in almost all my sequences, film director Sam Peckinpah gets a look-in too, as does another perennial favourite, the list poem. My archipelago is naturally inhabited by iguanas and giant tortoises, animals that have fascinated me all my life.

If this sounds like a somewhat predictable amalgamation of preoccupations and poetic tropes, I hope that is more than offset by the emotional currents that run through the poems and which are felt most strongly towards the end. I do sometimes wonder, if a poem doesn't move one to laughter or tears, what it's really worth. And yet I didn't set out to write about the loss of my daughter Lara earlier this year, nor about loneliness as such; the theme emerged as if of its own accord. The 'Bali Ha'i' song from the musical *South Pacific* perhaps nudged me in that direction, and the fact that I had a serious, extended bout of Covid illness while writing possibly played its part.

There is, then, an element of autobiographical material in the mix, but I have also—in the spirit of 'authorised theft'—borrowed detail from others' experience (and poems), and invented pretty wildly, sometimes in close proximity to historical fact. The flux within which these various elements, including time itself, co-exist is fundamental to my poetic enquiry.

JEN WEBB

This set of prose poems travels right around the Southern Ocean, moving from cape to island to the Antarctic continent along the Antarctic Convergence, and returning to where it starts: at the foot of Africa. I have never been to Antarctica, but started my life on the edge of what is now, though it was not then, the Southern Ocean; and have lived on continents and islands in its embrace for most of my life.

The Southern Ocean was only named as such in 2000, when the International Hydrographic Organization designated it an ocean, with somewhat fluid borders. Generally, it's considered to start at about 60°S; but various maps and other accounts describe its northern boundary by a sweep across the map that touches the base of South America (c.55°S), Australia (c.40°S), and Africa (c.35°S).[19]

Rather charmingly, the Southern Ocean is considered a concept rather than a geographic region, because its only 'real' boundary is the Antarctic Circumpolar Current, which flows, continuously, clockwise around Antarctica.[20] This current is a key agent in the regulation of global oceanic and climatic patterns. It connects the Atlantic, Indian, and Pacific Oceans and, by transporting cold water from the Southern Ocean to lower latitudes, it influences regional and global climate systems, maintaining temperatures and adding nutrients. It has served as an important carbon sink, but anthropogenic climate change is beginning to overwhelm its ability to maintain this role.[21]

The Southern Ocean is still largely unexplored, largely because of its extreme conditions. It is characterised by frigid temperatures, huge icebergs, and winds so powerful that they have attracted ludicrously dramatic names: the

---

[19] Most of my poems obediently locate themselves from 60°S and lower, but I have taken the liberty of touching on the various capes and islands that are included in the maps of the Antarctic region.
[20] Talley, LD, GL Pickard, WJ Emery and JH Swift (2011) *Descriptive Physical Oceanography: An introduction* (6th Edition), St Louis, MO: Elsevier.
[21] Marsh, R, and E van Sebille (2021) *Ocean Currents*, Amsterdam: Elsevier.

Roaring Forties, the Furious Fifties, the Screaming Sixties. It is home to very few humans, but to vast populations of krill; to orca and seals and the tough southern dolphins; many species of penguins and albatrosses, sharks and squids, nematodes and nudibranchs. It is home, too, to deep sea dwellers: ice fish, feather stars, basket stars, isopods et al.

It is a remarkable part of the world, and one that is vital to ecological health. This, alongside my personal obsession with the great Southern waters and all the wild weather and water patterns associated with them, compelled me to claim this ocean as mine, for the purposes of our 2023 collection. What I am trying to do in this sequence is to gesture toward the beauty and the alien qualities of this part of the world; to remind myself that humans really don't belong everywhere, but are just one small—if profoundly damaging—element of life's manifestations on earth. The ocean doesn't even notice us in our individual incursions into its domain, and hence its extreme danger to humans (especially those undomesticated oceans like the Arctic and the Southern); but *en masse* we are dealing death to all five oceans, all the seas, all the beautiful and fragile balance of the planet. Might poetry, that slow art, encourage us to pause, and reflect on our human responsibilities and remind us that the oceans are where we all began?

ABOUT THE POETS

CASSANDRA ATHERTON is an award-winning prose poet and leading scholar of prose poetry. She was a Visiting Scholar in English at Harvard University and a Visiting Fellow in Literature at Sophia University, Tokyo. Her most recent books of prose poetry are *Leftovers* (2020) and the co-written *Fugitive Letters* (2020). Cassandra co-wrote *Prose Poetry: An Introduction* (Princeton UP, 2020) and co-edited *The Anthology of Australian Prose Poetry* (Melbourne UP, 2020) with Paul Hetherington. They are currently writing *Ekphrastic Poetry: An Introduction* (Princeton UP, forthcoming). Cassandra is co-host of the international poetry livestream reading series, *LitBalm* and associate editor at MadHat Press (USA).

OZ HARDWICK is a European poet and academic, whose work has washed up on many shores. He has published a dozen or so full collections and chapbooks, including *Learning to Have Lost* (IPSI, 2018) which won the 2019 Rubery International Book Award for poetry, and most recently, *A Census of Preconceptions* (SurVision, 2022). He grew up in a thriving port which is now nothing but expensive holiday homes, and although he now lives 35 miles from the sea, he can still hear mermaids singing. Oz is Professor of Creative Writing at Leeds Trinity University, whose crest is a ship beneath bright stars. www.ozhardwick.co.uk

PAUL HETHERINGTON has published 17 full-length collections of poetry, including *Ragged Disclosures* (Recent Work Press, 2022) and *Her One Hundred and Seven Words* (MadHat Press, 2021), and his poetry has won or been nominated for more than 40 national and international awards and competitions. He has also written numerous academic chapters and articles. He founded International Poetry Studies at the University in Canberra in 2013 and is also co-founding editor of the journal *Axon: Creative Explorations*. In 2014 he founded the international Prose Poetry Group. With Cassandra Atherton, he co-authored *Prose Poetry: An Introduction* (Princeton UP, 2020) and co-edited the *Anthology of Australian Prose Poetry* (Melbourne UP, 2020).

PAUL MUNDEN is a poet, editor and screenwriter living in North Yorkshire. A Gregory Award winner, he has published six poetry collections, the latest of which is *Amplitude* (Recent Work Press, 2022). He was director of the UK's National Association of Writers in Education, 1994–2018, and a Royal Literary Fund Fellow at the University of Leeds, 2019–2023. He is an Adjunct Associate Professor at the University of Canberra, where he was director of Poetry on the Move, 2015–2017. His book *Unclassified: Nigel Kennedy in Chapters & Verse* will be published by Recent Work Press in 2024.
https://paulmunden.com

JEN WEBB is Distinguished Professor of Creative Practice, and Interim Dean of the Faculty of Arts and Design at the University of Canberra. Recent books include *Art and Human Rights: Contemporary Asian Contexts* (Manchester UP, 2016), *Gender and the Creative Labour Market* (Palgrave, 2022), and the poetry collections *Moving Targets* (Recent Work Press, 2018) and *Flight Mode* (with Shé Hawke; Recent Work Press, 2020). She is co-editor of the literary journal *Meniscus* and the scholarly journal *Axon: Creative Explorations*. Her scholarly work focuses on the ethics of representation, and on the field of creative practice; her poetry focuses on material poetics and questions of seeing and being.

IPSI: INTERNATIONAL POETRY STUDIES

International Poetry Studies (IPSI) is part of the Centre for Creative and Cultural Research, Faculty of Arts and Design, University of Canberra. IPSI conducts research related to poetry, and publishes and promulgates the outcomes of this research internationally. It also publishes poetry and interviews with poets, as well as related material, from around the world. Publication of such material takes place in IPSI's online journal *Axon: Creative Explorations* (www.axonjournal.com.au) and through other publishing vehicles. IPSI's goals include working—collaboratively, where possible—for the appreciation and understanding of poetry, poetic language and the cultural and social significance of poetry. IPSI also organises festivals, symposia, seminars, readings and other poetry related activities and events.

CCCR: CENTRE FOR CREATIVE AND CULTURAL RESEARCH

The Centre for Creative and Cultural Research (CCCR) is IPSI's umbrella organisation and brings together staff, adjuncts, research students and visiting fellows who work on key challenges within the cultural sector and creative field. A central feature of its research concerns the effects of digitisation and globalisation on cultural producers, whether individuals, communities or organisations.

www.ingramcontent.com/pod-product-compliance
Lightning Source LLC
Chambersburg PA
CBHW072006290426
44109CB00018B/2156